MENTOR X

MENTOR X

The Life-Changing Power
of Extraordinary Mentors

S<small>TEPHANIE</small> W<small>ICKOUSKI</small>

Beard Books

Published by Beard Books, Washington, D.C.

Cover design by PROSPER Creative Design

ISBN 978-1-58798-700-7

www.beardbooks.com

About this book:

This book is a stockpile of practical tips, stories, interviews, workbooks, ideas, and warnings. It is intentionally organized in segments and can be read in any order or at any pace the reader desires.

About my pronouns:

My use of "him" "her" "his" and "hers" is intended to be non-gender specific. "Him" and "her" are used interchangeably in this book as gender neutral and non-binary pronouns, i.e., the use of each of these pronouns is intended to refer to a person of any gender.

Disclaimers:

This book is intended as a practical resource. Its purpose is to provide useful information on the subject. It is not intended by the publisher or author as legal or other professional advice or service. The views expressed are that of the author's only and do not necessarily reflect the views of her firm or any other organization with which she is affiliated.

All stories, names, characters, and incidents described in this book are fictitious. No identification with actual persons (living or deceased), places, buildings, and products is intended or should be inferred.

To Roger Frankel

pro • té • gé

noun: one who is guided or protected or whose career is
                 furthered by a more experienced prominent, or
                 influential person

synonyms: pupil, student, scholar, apprentice, disciple, follower,
                 ward, charge.

                 circa 1965; mentee; *archaic*; fosterling

TABLE OF CONTENTS

PREFACE

This book was an unusual and unexpected venture for me. It started with a series of blog posts I wrote about my own search for a new mentor. It soon became apparent that the subject of mentors warranted a book. I had written two books on bankruptcy law, but writing about mentors was completely new for me.

I ran into obstacles at every turn. Some people saw the subject as already exhausted. Thus, I surveyed the popular literature on the subject to see whether, in fact, everything about mentors was already written.

My first impression of the existing literature was that it was dull, pedantic, and trite. Nothing I read seemed authentic. The mentoring construct described was stereotyped and clichéd. It did not at all resemble my personal experiences, or those of anyone I knew, with mentors.

The vast coverage of this subject also had another thing in common: it was written from the perspective of the mentors. Missing was the real-life perspective of the protégés. The coverage stayed in the comfort zone of the mentors. The dark, disturbing issues that sometimes surface in the course of mentor–protégé relationships — bias, exploitation, rivalry, harassment, corruption, and sex — were not touched. No one described what actually happens in these relationships and what separates the transformative ones from the ordinary. No one provided a roadmap for a protégé to tell a great mentor from a terrible one.

I set out to write about everything that was absent from all of the other literature: the things that no one else tells you about having a mentor, from the point of view of a protégé. Part 1 describes what a mentor is. Part 2 distinguishes a mentor from a teacher, coach, role model, buddy, or boss, and describes how a mentor can dramatically change the course of a protégé's life. Part 3 describes the qualities to look for in a mentor. Part 4 chronicles various types of mentors, including bold mentors, charismatic mentors, cold and distant mentors, dissolute mentors, personally bonded mentors, younger mentors, and unexpected mentors. Part 5 provides charts and workbooks to make is easier to get the most out of having a mentor. Part 6 describes the dark side of mentors, including boundary-crossing, rivalry, corruption, and other signs that the mentor relationship has run its course. Parts 7 and 8 contain Q&As, including interviews with protégés, their critiques of their mentors, and mentor–protégé nuts and bolts.

The book provides tips for dealing with all kinds of mentors — from great ones to difficult, corrupt, or even dysfunctional ones.

My provenance, New York City, is full of aspiring actors who want to be on Broadway someday. They work very hard and get by on very little while pursuing their dreams. One woman quit her job to take a small role with a director whom, she felt, could position her for a Broadway role. She saw the director as a real mentor and had absolute faith in him. Some of her colleagues were doubtful, however, that this was actually going to pan out. One of her particularly wary friends commented, "Everybody thinks they are going to be the next Megan Hilty." A year later, she was cast in the lead role of a Broadway show. In other words, she *did* become "the next Megan Hilty." It was not just her positivity, determination, and talent (which many people have), but having the right mentor (which most people do not have), that made this happen.

I strongly believe that having a true mentor dramatically affects a career and virtually assures a protégé's success. Nothing else in life carries a warranty as good as this. But the key is a real, true, great mentor — not a pseudo mentor, a bad mentor, or a false mentor. This book will help you find the right one, avoid the wrong ones, and set you firmly on the path to your most successful career.

ACKNOWLEDGMENTS

Many people inspired me to write this book and I am grateful to all of them.

My own terrific mentors.

My great publisher, Peter Chapman of Beard Books, and his mentor Christopher Beard.

My husband and creative co-conspirator, David Fletcher, who once again responded to a paper avalanche with enthusiasm and encouragement.

My sister, Sheila Wickouski, herself a published author, who first taught me to write and helped me with advice along the way.

My colleague, editor, writing coach, and friend, Howard Rogatnick, who made immeasurable contributions to the development of this book.

My terrific administrative assistant, Jeannette Lugo.

My friends and colleagues who provided ideas, including Shirley Cho, Jeremy Finkelstein, William Hibsher, Carol Hoshall, Veronica Mainetti, Martin Paisner, Isaac Sasson, and Melinda Wang.

Last and not least, my revered committee — Anthony, Therese and JT — who responded to my every request, no matter how difficult, ordinary, or hopeless.

ABOUT THE AUTHOR

Stephanie Wickouski is an American bankruptcy lawyer. A partner with the New York City office of Bryan Cave Leighton Paisner LLP, she has practiced bankruptcy law for more than 35 years, litigating complex reorganization cases throughout the country and serving as lead bankruptcy counsel in multiple high-profile cases, including *Energy Future, iHeartmedia, Windstream, Seadrill, Caesars Entertainment, United Airlines, Northwest Airlines, General Maritime, General Motors, Hayes Lemmerz, ION Media, Escada, Bally Total Fitness, Dex Media, New Page, Independence Air, Loral Orion, USGen New England, Tower Automotive, WHX Corp., Armstrong World Industries,* and *Friendly Restaurants.*

Named in *New York Super Lawyers* and *The Best Lawyers in America* year after year, she is a well-known presence in the national bankruptcy community. She has been named as one of the 12 Outstanding Restructuring Lawyers in the U.S. by *Turnarounds & Workouts.* She is the author of two other books, *Bankruptcy Crimes* (3rd Ed.) (Beard Books), the leading authoritative treatise on bankruptcy crime, and *Indenture Trustee Bankruptcy Powers & Duties* (Beard Books 2015), a practical guide for the distressed debt industry, as well as the *Corporate Restructuring Blog.* (http://blogs.bankrupt.com/).

Stephanie Wickouski can be reached at swickouski@gmail.com.

PART 1
The X Factor

PART 1:

The X Factor

1.1 Mentor X

In mathematics, X is the name for an independent variable or unknown factor. X is also used as the multiplication factor.

Malcolm X adopted X as his last name as a symbol of rejecting the name of his ancestors' enslavers and forging an independent identity.

In art or fashion, the use of X indicates an influential collaboration by two or more individuals or companies, e.g., Stella McCartney x adidas.

X is transformative. Apple chose "X" to follow the iPhone 8 — skipping over 9 — to mark a dramatic innovation.

X refers to a quality (as in the "X Factor") that is hard to define — yet at the same time, defining.

This is what a mentor does. A mentor leads you to find your unknown factor. A mentor multiplies the qualities you have and what you can do. A mentor inspires a rejection of the past and the forging of a new, independent identity. A mentor brings about a powerful collaboration. A mentor is transformative. A mentor is defining, yet hard to define.

Mentor X may be known to you, or may be someone you have yet to meet.

This book is about Mentor X.

1.2 Letter to a future protégé

Dear Stacey,

I am writing this letter to you because I know how much uncertainty you feel right now. You go through a couple of weeks of feeling that your career is on track; then something hits you out of nowhere and makes you question everything. You wonder if you are going in the right direction, or if you are doomed to fail.

This roller-coaster feeling will never completely go away.

I wish I could help you. All I can do is leave you this book in hopes it will serve as a navigation app.

It's impossible for you to see your potential — what you are capable of achieving. You are in the center of your life, so you can't see it objectively. Moreover, you are bombarded with external data from all directions. Your intuition becomes drowned out by the voices of other people.

Other people see you through their own prism, and their view is not objective. There are a few people who see you clearly. In that pool of people, you may find a real advisor — a mentor — someone who will make it his mission to be a sounding board and give you good advice.

I want you to feel hopeful about what lies ahead, but there is only so much I can do. You have to find your Mentor X. He will take it from there.

Very best,
Stephanie

1.3 What a mentor can do

I had an associate who adopted me as her mentor. She was brilliant and exceptional. Being a mentor to her was — as the saying goes — a piece of cake.

One Mother's Day, she brought me a plant. The note said, "Happy Mother's Day to my mentor. Because a mentor is like a mother."

These were lovely words and I have never forgotten them. Even if they are completely untrue.

A mentor is not like a mother. Nor is she like a teacher, a coach, or a boss. She is not an authority figure. A true mentor may tell a protégé to ignore the teacher, leave the coach, or defy the boss. For many reasons to be discussed throughout this book, it's preferable to have a mentor who is not your teacher, coach, or boss, as each of these relationships may conflict with the role of a mentor.

A mentor does not have to be a role model. A mentor can be deeply flawed and set a bad example in many areas of his life. There are both kinds of mentors — the role models and the flawed. Part 4 discusses the various types of mentors and how to get the most from each.

Not everything that a mentor says is right. You need to be able to separate truth from nonsense.

Not everything a mentor "is" is right, either. Mentors can be cold and distant. They can be dysfunctional. They can have addictions. They can be corrupt or unethical. But they all have one thing in common: they tell you the things that you don't know, that you absolutely need to know, and that no one else is telling you. In fact, when deciding who to adopt as a mentor, this point is one that you must not compromise.

A mentor does not need to be older than you. You can have a younger mentor. In fact, if you are old enough that your mentors are dead, you may benefit from having a new mentor who is younger — maybe even a lot younger. A younger mentor and an older mentor might sometimes have different perspectives, yet the essential qualities of being a mentor do not depend on age.

What can a mentor do for you?

You go through most of your life in the confused zone, without even realizing what clarity is like. A mentor leads you to clarity.

A mentor does not have to do that much, but what he does is life-changing.

When you are in the fog, being led out of it by a mentor, you may not even be aware of what is happening. In fact, the experience may be so much "in the moment" that you may not realize what has occurred until many years later.

PART 2

The Backstory

PART 2:

The Backstory

2.1 What is a mentor?

Mentors are not what they used to be.

The original "Mentor" was, in fact, an imposter. In Homer's *Odyssey*, Athena, the goddess of wisdom and courage, disguised herself as another character (Mentor) and in that disguise, gave counsel to Telemachus. The actual "Mentor" was not up to the task of providing the counsel. Conversely, Telemachus did not realize he was getting advice straight from Athena.

This story is illuminating to those in search of a mentor now. Mentors are not always who you think they are.

The word "mentor" — like the word "genius" — has been overused and misused to the point of becoming practically meaningless. "Mentor" has devolved in current usage to include a teacher, buddy, role model, confidante, big brother, coach, or boss. While any of these may potentially be mentors (or geniuses, for that matter), none of those roles defines what a mentor is.

A teacher is someone who imparts knowledge and helps you to learn core competency.

A coach is someone who acts as a trainer and helps you practice to hone skills.

A buddy is someone who shows you the ropes and helps you acclimate to the office.

A role model is someone who embodies the qualities you admire and whose example you want to follow.

A sponsor is someone who advocates for your advancement.

A mentor may also be one of the foregoing (or may be none of them). A mentor, at the most basic level, is a trusted advisor — a guru. But a true mentor — a "Mentor X" — is much more than that.

A mentor is someone who sees, understands, and accepts your calling, without trying to superimpose his own values or agenda. A mentor may identify with you in some respects, but must not see you as a reflection of himself. A mentor must be someone who has the unique ability to see what you specifically need to move ahead — what you do not know or are not able to see for yourself. Most of all, a mentor has to be willing to give you unsolicited advice that is reliable and truthful. This last part is rarer than you might think.

Gil Scott-Heron wrote, "Good advice is sure enough hard to come by. Bad advice is easy, because it's free." This was written as a lyrical line, not for literal truth. It is, nevertheless, somewhat true. Mass-produced, generic advice (which describes most of the career advice published on the internet, discussed in Chapter 3.5) is easy and free, often inadequate, and sometimes wrong. The rare, individualized advice of a true mentor, on the other hand, is hard to come by, and, while it may be free, it is often not easy.

Having a true mentor will enable you to resist the temptation to take piecemeal advice from random people. Some of this advice might not be so good. Simply because advice is from your teacher, boss, or coach, does not mean that the advice is right, or right for you. Often, such people do not know you well enough to give you the best advice. Their advice may be objectively "good" and well-intended. But it may be the wrong advice for *you*. Such advice might even be disastrous if you were to follow it. Where important, career-determinative advice is concerned, you need to be selective in who you listen to and who you follow.

As a child, you were probably taught to color, using a coloring book. You were given crayons with the expectation that you would use certain colors for a given picture — for example, brown for the bark of a tree, and green for the leaves. If you used cerulean for a tree's bark, you were probably corrected. A mentor is a person who, figuratively speaking, tells you that cerulean is just fine for a tree. In fact, a real mentor might actually suggest it.

A contemporary clothing brand, targeting young women, ran an Instagram ad showing a girl in a short skirt, with the caption: "That moment when you realize you're the bad influence." Of course, the ad is using the word "bad" to mean really, really good. A true mentor will help you realize that you are the "bad" influence. He will encourage that part of you that wants to color outside the lines, or use unconventional colors. Most importantly, he will open up a door to a part of the world that is using cerulean as the color of trees — a "world" you never realized existed until you had a mentor.

A mentor will see your dreams and the full range of your possibilities in ways that you cannot. He may give you specific advice — to apply for a certain job, undertake a given project, or focus on a particular area. He might give you advice that is bold and controversial. For example, he may urge you to move an entire industry in a radically new direction. Things that you never thought possible, seem attainable when suggested by a mentor. A true mentor will make you think of yourself and your career in a dramatically expansive way.

Specific advice from a mentor can propel a protégé's career in a dramatic direction. Prior to the Bankruptcy Reform Act of 1978, bankruptcy judges did not have law clerks. In 1979, perhaps only a handful of law professors perceived that there would be many new judicial clerkship opportunities in the field of bankruptcy law for new graduates. My law school dean had worked on the congressional commission that drafted the law, and he knew many of the bankruptcy judges through his work on the commission. One of my earliest mentors, he opened doors for me to a federal judicial clerkship, which became the first step in launching my career in bankruptcy law.

In Part 3, you will get tips for finding a true mentor and learn easy ways to tell whether advice is good or bad.

There are numerous types of mentors, each with transformative power. Part 4 will survey some of these types.

Mentors must be non-paying relationships. There is an entire cottage industry of professional coaches who will come at me with pitchforks for this. Coaches may have value, but they are not mentors. Why? Because a mentor is not a "girlfriend experience."

The cable network series, *The Girlfriend Experience*, is about a female escort who provides an experience that blurs the boundaries between a financial transaction and an authentic romantic encounter. The series is based on a 2009 movie of the same name directed by Steven Soderbergh, with Sasha Grey in the lead role of Chelsea, an escort who provides a "girlfriend experience." There is a famous scene in the movie where Chelsea tells a friend that her clients are not "real" relationships. She contrasts this with her relationship with her boyfriend, a relationship based not on a financial transaction, but on a genuine emotional connection.

The financial nature of relationship with a coach destroys its authenticity as a true mentoring relationship. Mentors — like "real" girlfriends — are real relationships.

2.2 Is a mentor really necessary?

In the course of writing this book, several people told me that they never had a mentor, and haven't missed anything. This has led me to ask the question: Is a mentor really necessary?

The answer is: it depends.

Navigating a career without the right mentor is like hiking in the wilderness without a compass. If you don't mind being lost, a compass isn't necessary.

Without a mentor, you will be lost for a long time, maybe permanently. Having a true mentor is a rare human experience which is the critical dividing point between success and failure.

It can't just be any mentor. The choice of mentor is one of the most important decisions in a person's life.

There are points in your life where you need good advice, and you need a mentor to give it.

Without a Mentor X, your life will be a lot harder than it has to be. A Mentor X is a silver bullet. With a Mentor X, your success is virtually guaranteed.

Is this hyperbole? No. This book will introduce you to the rarely traveled world of the authentic mentor experience.

What can a mentor do for you that you can't do for yourself? After all, a mentor just gives a little guidance. This may not even involve that much time spent. Mentors have a range of involvement in their protégés' lives. Some have very little contact — a text here and there — where others may practically spend every waking hour with their protégé. There are different ways in which a mentor might give you guidance.

A mentor will jolt you into action in a way that no one else can. Mentors set a direction. This is the "Zen" of the mentoring relationship, the lightning bolt of advice that can change the course of a career.

This is harder than it sounds.

Over time, you may actually need several mentors. One expectation of mentors in the legal profession is to bring about an understanding of how courts, lawyers, clients, financial advisors, investment bankers, capital markets, regulators, and, at times, academia, all work together to form the legal and economic system. Such an understanding is not conveyed in a couple of sound bites or texts, but is built tediously over months or years. In fact, the "technologies" (legal, financial, and strategic) evolve so fast, almost at an exponential rate, that the need for guidance is never ending.

One reason why you may need more than one mentor is that the kind of advice you need will change over the course of your career, as both you and the world around you change exponentially. To paraphrase the popular expression, the mentor you may need now or in the future is "not your mother's mentor." Quite possibly, your mentor may be younger.

Mentors sometimes cease to be mentors. The book will show you how to recognize when someone is no longer your mentor, and how to replace him when that occurs.

2.3 A mentor is a visionary

A mentor is a visionary — he sees the protégé and his potential in a way that no one else might see it. A mentor sees pathways forward that a protégé is incapable of seeing himself. Only if a mentor has this vision is he able to give accurate advice.

A mentor must see *you*. This is not as simple as it sounds.

I have a personal confession, an instance in which I failed as a mentor. Julia, an associate in another large law firm, was a tremendously talented, accomplished, and credentialed lawyer, having been educated at Princeton, Oxford, and Yale. We spoke a lot about her career goals. I felt she had a brilliant future as a lawyer.

Julia expressed chronic dissatisfaction with her situation. Every time she said she wasn't happy, I said the same thing: "Why not change firms?" She eventually took my advice and interviewed at a number of firms. After eventually changing firms, she still expressed the same unhappiness. My advice (again) was: "Why not change firms?"

Fortunately, this time, Julia completely disregarded my advice. She left the law completely to open an art gallery. After she had made the move, we met for drinks. She looked radiant – more energized and upbeat than I had ever seen her. I told her that I felt I had failed her as a friend and mentor, because I had not really understood or listened to her. I had simply superimposed my own assumption — that everyone is as enthusiastic about the law as I am. She said, "Don't feel bad. Every time you said 'why not change firms,' you made me realize that I didn't want to practice law."

I had failed to see that the law was not Julia's calling. I had failed to see Julia.

Some people can spend hundreds of hours with you and still not really know you. Others can have limited contact with you and understand everything about you. But this is key: if a mentor doesn't really understand you, he will not be able to give good advice. He may offer ideas, but they will be hit-or-miss. He may try to open doors for you, but they may be the wrong doors.

Every time I said to Julia, "Why not change firms?" it was a sign that I didn't really "see" her — that I was not her mentor.

How do you know when a mentor really "sees" you?

Jill, a young litigation partner in a large law firm, had a colleague, Doug, who was a successful senior partner in the litigation group in her firm. Doug's office was next to Jill's, and she found herself frequently talking to him about issues in the firm and dilemmas she was facing with clients and in the practice of law generally. She found Doug to be a source of common-sense advice (something not so common at all).

One day, when they were talking about their respective children, Doug said to Jill, "I imagine that when you were a little girl, you had long curly blond hair, you wore a tiara and looked like a little princess." Jill was taken aback by Doug's comment. In fact, as a child, she was a tomboy and sometimes even mistaken for a boy. Her hair was short, and during much of her childhood, she had a buzz cut. Recognizing that her daughter was not a "girly" girl, Jill's mother dressed her in pants and shorts instead of dresses. Once, Jill was given a pink, ruffled dress by a well-meaning aunt who was trying to encourage Jill's feminine side. Young Jill refused to wear the dress, not even wanting to try it on, so her mother eventually gave it away. That Doug would see Jill as having been a "princess-like" little girl was proof that Doug did not really know her. While she still considered Doug's advice, she started questioning whether his advice was actually relevant to *her*. She realized that Doug — a great colleague and friend — was not her mentor.

When someone who you think may be your mentor misses the mark completely and fails to "see" you, you will know it unmistakably.

2.4 Dementors

In her *Harry Potter* novels, J.K. Rowling describes beings that are powerful, dark, and highly destructive. When these beings attack, they remove a person's happiness, hope, and ambition. These beings are called "dementors." The only cure for an attack by dementors is — apparently — chocolate.

Of course, dementors do not actually exist. However, there are real dementing influences that can have the same effect on a person's career. Unlike the dementors in the *Harry Potter* books, these dementors are very real — they are just not corporeal. These "dementors" are fear, doubt, and greed, and they can take away hope, direction, and happiness.

One indication of a true mentor is someone who counteracts the three dementors. A mentor emboldens you, so fear is dispelled. A mentor builds your faith, driving away doubt. A mentor fuels your drive, not your greed.

How does a mentor do these things? A friend of mine, Amy, says that her mentor, Scott, showed her the art, as opposed to the science, of law practice. Scott clued Amy in to the secret ways of getting things done. He opened doors that she never knew existed — for example, recommending her for slots on panels of various industry and trade associations. Through these groups, Amy made contacts who could support her selection as counsel. As she got more traction as a panelist and speaker, Scott spread the word to other partners throughout the country, and they, in turn, helped Amy get on more panels, including international ones. She, in turn, developed more contacts for a growing practice. Amy is a natural: she jumped at the chance to hop on a plane, speak on a panel, and meet new people. Scott saw this quality in her, and encouraged it.

A pseudo-mentor may have encouraged Amy to take on a project that was not right for her at this point in her career, for example, getting on a team working on a Supreme Court brief. While such a project has objective merit, it would not have inspired Amy or turbocharged her career. Activities such as this may even have proved to be "dementors" in themselves, creating doubt as to her love of the law or draining her ambition. Scott, a true mentor to Amy, opened exactly the right doors for her to realize her own highest and best use.

A mentor is someone who fortifies you against the influence of dementors. A mentor dispels fear, doubt, and greed. A mentor fuels ambition and brings hope and happiness.

As in the legal profession, in many industries there are a lot of doors. Some are hidden. Many are locked. Without a mentor, you can find yourself lost, or behind a locked door (like Harry Potter in any number of situations). In the real world, there are no "spells" like Harry Potter used to ward off dementors or to unlock doors. To practice magic in the real world, you need the help of a mentor.

2.5 Tormentors

Tormentors are the human, corporeal analogue of dementors: carriers of fear, doubt, greed.

Tormentors include people who threaten you with retaliation or punishment when you stand up for what is right, whether for yourself or others. Tormentors may threaten you directly or indirectly. There are tormentors who threaten you physically, such as harassers at work. Such harassers range from angry bosses who throw objects (like trash cans or books) at their subordinates, to predators who grab and grope their co-workers.

Tormentors include people who cause you to question yourself, whether it is your knowledge, ability, or personality. Some ways that a tormentor may do this is by making "observations" about you that, while seeming innocent on their face, are unflattering or unsettling. This type of tormentor — a passively hostile one — can be the most dangerous.

Tormentors also include people who make you feel insecure financially or fuel competitive material desires, such as people who flaunt their real estate, cars, vacations, or acquisitions.

Tormentors fuel the dementors of fear, doubt, and greed.

Tormentors are everywhere. It's impossible to escape them. They are at work, at school, at church.

The influence of a mentor can insulate you from the harm of a tormentor. A mentor's counsel operates like a force field. A mentor can give you skills to immunize yourself from the effects of tormentors. If a tormentor is physically threatening, a mentor will counsel you on how to report the abuse and protect yourself from retaliation in the process. A mentor can give you words and techniques to stop a tormentor dead in his tracks and keep him from menacing you again.

2.6 Seven things no one tells you about having a mentor

A mentor may not teach you anything (but you will learn a lot).

A mentor will show you how things get done and how things really are.

You will get insights about yourself. You will recognize strengths that a mentor will identify and which you may not be aware of in yourself.

Three men were extremely influential in my legal career and professional development: the judge I clerked for, my branch chief at the Department of Justice, and a senior partner in a prior law firm, yet I don't consider any of them to have been mentors. These three individuals taught me most of my basic substantive knowledge and legal skills, for which I owe each a debt of gratitude. I consider them teachers, but not mentors.

My mentors, on the other hand, didn't teach me much in the way of substantive skills. Instead, they showed me secrets that I could learn nowhere else. They showed me how doors are opened. They showed me how to be an agent of change and advance innovative and controversial ideas. These are the kinds of things that true mentors do, the kinds of things that only a mentor can do for you.

A mentor can show you the inside track.

A mentor shows you the secrets of the industry that are not written down anywhere. Some would call this "how to get in the back door when you can't get in the front door."

A real mentor will bring you joy.

A real mentor sees you as you really are and not as a reflection of himself. A mentor will make you see your strengths, strengths that you may not see in yourself. A mentor will open a door to your future that you did not know existed.

All of this will make you hopeful, positive, and — yes — happy.

A mentor can get too close.

It's important to have a healthy boundary between you and your mentor.

There are some protégés who have exceptionally close relationships with their mentors, especially when the mentor is in the same firm or company as the protégé. They may have lunch with their mentor every day, visit their mentor's house, or their families may vacation together. Some even cross the boundary of a physical relationship with their mentors.

While such closeness does not always impair a good mentor–protégé relationship, it does complicate it. This is because boundaries are important when a mentor is acting in the capacity as a mentor. If the mentor is too close, how do you distinguish life-changing, "mentor" advice from dinner conversation — or, for that matter, pillow talk?

One successful woman lawyer clerked for a famous federal judge, who later became her mentor, and eventually her husband. He was a great boss, mentor, and husband to her. His roles as boss, mentor, and husband were not simultaneous, but consecutive. For most people, however, relationships cannot be so cleanly compartmentalized.

The reality TV show, *90 Day Fiancé*, is about Americans who are marrying immigrants with K-1 visas. The couples have many challenges and conflicts, including conflicts over their respective careers. In one episode, Russ, from Oklahoma, objected to his wife Paola, from Columbia, working as a lingerie model. Russ was uncomfortable about Paola being seen and photographed in her underwear. Paola sought her mother's advice as to how to resolve the conflict between her desire to pursue a modeling career and her husband's disapproval.

Paola's mother came down squarely on the side of career, saying to Paola: "It's easier to change husbands than to change jobs."

In a situation where there is an overlap between mentor and lover, the question becomes: which is easier to change? If neither, then both you and your mentor have to agree on some ground rules about your overlapping relationships. Ironically, the closer you are, the less awkward it is to have a conversation about compartmentalizing your overlapping relationships. Without this, however — like Paola and Russ — there will likely be ongoing conflicts. Without establishing boundaries, both the mentoring relationship and the personal relationship will suffer.

> **Note:** *Many organizations have rules governing or even prohibiting certain close relationships between employees. There are important legal and policy reasons for these rules, which override other considerations.*

A mentor will make you double down on who you really are.

There is a sign in a store in my neighborhood that reads, "What would you do if you knew you could not fail?" A mentor makes you do just that: what you would do if you knew you could not fail. He doesn't simply encourage you vaguely or blindly. He sees your specific potential — things that most everyone else fails to see. He recognizes your calling and leads you to follow it.

A mentor may not like you, but still be a great mentor.

Ralph Waldo Emerson, widely considered to be the mentor of Henry David Thoreau, actually found Thoreau annoying (as did almost everyone else), and probably sent him to Walden Pond to get rid of him. This opened a door for Thoreau to write the best work of his life.

While not the ideal situation, it's possible to have a great mentor who can't stand you, but still gives you good advice. Such a relationship might be conducted largely through emails or text, instead of face-to-face. If your mentor finds you annoying (or vice versa), electronic communications may neutralize the annoyance.

You must be able to communicate in some way with your mentor, whether by phone, text, email, or in person. A "mentor" who is generally inaccessible or who doesn't communicate well is not a mentor worth having, unless there are overwhelming pluses that outweigh his limitations.

Not everyone's mentoring relationship is out of a story book, in which the mentor is a warm and fuzzy, teddy-bear like presence. Some mentors are cold and distant, abrasive or eccentric. While this is not optimal and clearly makes the relationship more challenging, if it's the right mentor in crucial respects, you can learn to manage quirks or even defects of character.

A bad or false mentor is worse than no mentor at all.

The search for a mentor carries the risk of ending up with a bad or a false mentor.

A bad mentor is one who does not help you or give you good advice, and who might even give you bad advice. A bad mentor sees you as an extension of himself. His advice misses the mark because it is relevant only to him, not to you.

A bad mentor can be dangerous. If a mentor advises you to take a bold or risky action (such as quitting a job, leaking an explosive story to the press, or confronting an authority figure) and the mentor's advice is wrong, either due to bad judgment or misunderstanding the situation, the result for the protégé could be disastrous. If the advice is bad enough, the damage might be irreparable.

If bad mentors aren't bad enough, there are also false mentors, which are even worse. A false mentor lures a protégé with the promise of helping him in his career, but the motives of the "mentor" are in fact to exploit, or even abuse, the protégé. The media is full of reports of young actresses, models and vocalists seeking guidance and help from celebrity producers and promoters. Some of these putative mentors have turned out to be predators, kidnappers, or rapists. A false mentor must be avoided at all costs.

2.7 Famous mentor–protégé relationships

- Socrates – Plato
- Plato – Aristotle
- George Washington – Alexander Hamilton
- Ralph Waldo Emerson – Henry David Thoreau
- Richard Wright – James Baldwin
- William O. Douglas – Abe Fortas
- Christian Dior – Yves Saint Laurent
- Dorothy Day – Daniel Berrigan
- Martin Luther King, Jr. – John Lewis
- James A. Porter – David Driskell
- David Driskell – Jefferson Pinder
- David Driskell – Ellington Robinson
- Ray Charles – Quincy Jones
- Maya Angelou – Oprah Winfrey
- E. Barrett Prettyman – John G. Roberts
- Warren Buffet – Bill Gates
- Steven Spielberg – JJ Abrams
- Larry Summers – Sheryl Sandberg
- Steve Jobs – Mark Zuckerberg

There are also famous fictional mentors:

- Obi-Wan Kenobi – Luke Skywalker
- Professor Dumbledore – Harry Potter
- Krishna (a/k/a Vishnu) – Arjuna
- Zuri – T'Challa

PART 3

Secrets and Lies

PART 3:

Secrets and Lies

3.1 Looking for Mentor X

The search for a mentor can be easy or hard. Like dating, some sign up for OkCupid and meet their future husband the same day. Others delete their accounts after months of bad dates.

You've gotten this far in the book and have decided you want and need a mentor. You're looking for transformative change — for the X factor. So what do you do now? Where or how will you find your mentor?

Chances are that you know your mentor already, but have not yet realized that he is your mentor.

3.2 The value of disruption

In some fields — law among them — there are traditional or built-in mentors, such as judges or senior partners in law firms. In other fields, finding a mentor may require networking or introductions to others in the industry in the quest for a mentor. Either way, finding a mentor may be hard. It may take time and effort. The time and effort will be worth it, however, assuming that you are prepared for what comes next.

Once you have a mentor, he will shake up your life more than you realize.

A mentor might make you question long-standing premises. A true mentor sees all your options as "on the table." A mentor may cause you to turn your life upside down. Having a mentor can lead to extreme disruption in your life.

Ask yourself: Do I value disruption? Is having a mentor worth having my life shaken up?

Fortunately, disruption is not the only thing a mentor brings. A mentor is not only a disruptor, but a sage.

A sage is someone who has attained wisdom. The modern equivalent of a sage is a "relevant elder" — a person who has great experience and judgment and is a source of good advice.

Sage is also an aromatic plant believed to have antiseptic properties. It is used for healing and "smudging," which means removing negative properties from a physical space.

A mentor is a sage, and also acts like sage. Like a sage, a mentor imparts wisdom and clarity. In the process of imparting wisdom, a mentor brings about a "space clearing" in your values and goals — making you get rid of the obsolete or useless ones, the ones you are hanging on to, like clutter in your house. You must ask yourself: are you ready to give up the clutter in your career that is holding you back, and to move forward, even if it creates disruption in your life?

3.3 Institutional mentoring programs

Over the past few years, many organizations have launched formal mentoring programs. In law firms, these programs may involve pairing associates with "mentors" or facilitating introductions by means such as "mentoring parties" where associates and partners can mingle. A few companies describe their programs as highly successful.

There is no doubt that these programs are successful at what they literally set out to do — connect senior and junior employees — and that they bring about positive results, including improved communication and collegiality. But they accomplish very little when it comes to mentoring.

There are several fairly obvious reasons why touted success is not a reliable indicator of these programs' efficacy at bringing about true mentor-protégé relationships. First, organizations measure their success at mentoring programs only by internal benchmarks, which might not be independent or scientific. Second, whether a mentoring relationship actually "works" in the sense of having a meaningful, positive impact on a person's career is not apparent until much later — possibly as much as 25 years later or more. Third, the feedback is often entirely from non-management employees (such as law firm associates) who work for the firm instituting the program, and may feel compelled to provide positive feedback.

Last, the inherent assumptions behind the programs are flawed. The first flawed assumption is that women and minorities need mentoring more than white men in order to succeed. There is a lack of hard data supporting this assumption, yet it remains an assumption in many organizations. For at least the past 50 years, much has been written about the existence of a mentor being a key to success for women — in fact, the existence of a mentor has been regarded as a common factor among successful women. Having a mentor was seen as the magic bullet for a woman to succeed, and the lack of a mentor was seen as the reason many women fail. Although it is hard to identify where this idea originated, it has become so much a part of the corporate collective unconscious that even to question it seems heretical.

Fortunately, there *are* such heretics, particularly in the last ten years, such as Herminia Ibarra of London Business School. In a 2010 *Harvard Business Review* podcast "Women Are Over-Mentored (But Under-Sponsored)," as well as works co-authored with Nancy Carter and Christine Silva, Ibarra posited that women are not under-mentored at all — they are under-sponsored. The same may be true for other minorities, and even for white men, who don't always have sponsors (or mentors, for that matter) and need them too. The issue of under-sponsoring is not addressed by traditional or typical mentor programs.

The other inherent and flawed assumption is that mentor–protégé relationships can be somehow externally established, assigned, or brokered by third parties. This is a mass deception. The program approach is actually antithetical to true mentoring. Programs might even retard the establishment of true mentoring relationships by ascribing a "mentoring" label to a buddy system or big sister arrangement. These may create the illusion that one has a mentor with the unfortunate result that the "mentee" will be less likely to look for, and bond with, a true mentor.

Mentoring programs miss the mark. Assigning or brokering mentors negates the most critical components of a true mentor–protégé relationship — the individual process of self-awareness which leads a person to recognize another individual who will give the advice singularly needed. That very process is undermined by having a mentor assigned or by going to a mentoring party.

No one ever met Mentor X at a mentoring party.

If there is any way to stop someone from seeking out a true mentor, it's to assign him a mentor. Even Chelsea's clients from Part 2 were able to select her and take steps to seek her out. This, of course, was not even a real relationship, much less a relationship as significant and life-changing as a mentor. Even the programs that allow associates to choose their own mentors can be constraining, because the relationship is labeled before it actually develops. This is the equivalent of the reality TV show *Married at First Sight* in which contestants are introduced to their spouse for the first time at the altar. The contestants agree to have the wedding before the courtship. Predictably, most of these pairings either fail or end up lacking some of the elements that most people want in a marriage.

How can an organization promote mentorship? Organizations that attract people with creativity and drive, and focus on professional growth throughout their employees' entire careers, are places where true mentor-protégé relationships are found.

In a September 3, 2016 *New York Times* article, "You're How Old? We'll Be in Touch," Ashton Applewhite cited the "shoe test": ". . .look under the table, and if everyone's wearing the same kind of shoes, whether wingtips or flip-flops, you've got a problem." Organizations that pass the "shoe test" are the most fertile environments in which to find a mentor.

Firms that foster true mentorship are filled with people who seek advice and people who are willing to give advice. Such organizations encourage collaboration and the sharing of ideas. A workplace in which mentor-protégé relationships will have the greatest chance to develop is one that is diverse and inclusive in all respects, including gender, sexual orientation, race, ethnicity, provenance, geography, economic background, and age. Above all, a firm that prizes and encourages creativity and diversity of thought will be one in which these relationships flourish.

3.4 Signs of a good mentor

The search for a mentor is the search for a good advisor that you can trust completely. How do you distinguish a good potential mentor from a bad one? Here are three tips to looking for a good mentor candidate.

A mentor's personal judgment matters, not his personal characteristics.

A mentor does not have to exemplify the life or career you aspire to (although it may help if he does). A mentor *does* have to have exceptional judgment when it comes to your life and career. Sometimes the signs that a person has great judgment in this respect can be hidden or subtle.

My three mentors were impeccably dressed men. All three were lawyers, but had not much else in common except for their bespoke suits and luxury accessories. I did not pay attention to any of this when each was my mentor. Only in retrospect did I realize that they all had certain traits in common: elegance, attention to detail, and exceedingly high standards. These qualities were reflected in their professional lives as well, although they had taken very different career paths.

What they had in common as mentors was their attention to detail, their great judgment, and their high expectations. Each was able to pay close attention to who I was and where I was going. Each had great judgment in the advice he gave me. Each believed that I could meet his highest standards.

A mentor must be someone who sees you clearly.

Everyone has a calling, the gravitational pull of a specific course of action, with the associated duties, conduct, and way of life. An individual's calling is like a fingerprint. It may resemble someone else's, but it is unique. A mentor is a real, personal visionary who will help you find and follow your calling. Finding and following that calling is more important than anything else in the course of a career.

A mentor is a person who envisions a protégé's calling and who has the judgement and devotion to guide the protégé toward it. There are pseudo mentors — guidance counselors, parents, coaches, motivational speakers — who may offer tidbits of useful information, but they are not unbiased seers of the calling. None of them are mentors.

A mentor communicates in a way that you understand and believe.

Sometimes a seemingly small or insignificant insight or piece of advice will change a course of a career forever. Other times, a great piece of advice can go completely ignored. Whether the advice is large or small, it will only be impactful if communicated in a way that is heard, understood, and believed.

If your mentor talks to you in a way that resonates with you, chances are you will remember his words. The chemistry between the two of you is often the best indication that your communication will be good. While the word "chemistry" is often used to mean a physical spark in a romantic relationship, chemistry of a different form exists in business or professional relationships as well. Chemistry is a sign of an intellectual connection that is key in a mentor–protégé relationship.

The Five Qualities of a True Mentor
1. *A true mentor sees your strengths that others do not see.*
2. *A true mentor gives you unsolicited advice.*
3. *A true mentor always tells you the truth.*
4. *A true mentor simultaneously sees the person you are, and the person you can become.*
5. *A true mentor knows when you don't need him.*

3.5 Crowdsourced mentoring

Some careers — law, medicine, investment banking, teaching — offer a natural environment for identifying and developing a relationship with a mentor. Many organizations such as law firms, physician groups, investment banks, and academic institutions encourage and facilitate mentor–protégé relationships. Other careers — entrepreneurship or the arts — exist outside of formal structures or institutions where potential mentors can be found. In particular, entrepreneurs who are trying to launch a start-up find themselves in search of someone to set a direction for them and jolt them into action. In the lonely world of the start-up, a muse, sage or relevant elder is not always in the immediate line of sight. The lack of immediate or easy access to a mentor leads some people to pursue a crowdsourcing approach.

There are numerous specific blogs, forums or message boards, and chat rooms for everything from solo law practice to launching an Etsy business. Posting questions seeking advice on a message board or internet forum is a form of crowdsourced mentoring. Another form, which requires much more initiative, is creating a blog about an individual business venture or other entrepreneurial initiative, and posting articles to solicit comments from strangers. Another particularly creative mode of crowdsourced mentoring is launching a YouTube channel.

Because forums and message boards are easy and fast, and do not require the time and energy needed to create a blog or channel, many who are in search of immediate advice will turn to a forum.

One of the biggest challenges of blogs and YouTube channels is drawing readers and attracting subscribers. If done successfully, and a large number of subscribers are obtained, the blog or channel can become an independent source of advertising income or other means of making a living. This may benefit the protégé financially, but neither subscribers nor advertisers are a reliable source of advice.

An internet forum can be seductive, even addicting. It can also produce strange, conflicting or bad advice. An example of this is a young lawyer (Autumn1998) who turned to a young women professionals' forum to ask what to wear to an interview at an Am Law 100 firm.

> **Autumn 1998:** Hey guys, I have an interview coming up for associate position at firm in NY. I am trying to decide what to wear and what bag to carry. I have a black suit with a short shirt, and black pumps. Should I wear this or is this all wrong? HELP!!

> **Journey 1990:** Hey Autumn1998 — that's great news! On the bag, be sure it's not a designer bag or anything too expensive. You don't want them to think you don't need the job. On the suit, I think a black suit and plain black pumps are great for a law firm interview.

> **Amber 1985:** Hi Autumn! I think you should carry the best bag you have — a high quality designer bag makes a good impression. On the suit, I would avoid black. Black can be harsh, funereal. Navy or grey is preferable. I'd also be careful about short skirts. If a female partner is interviewing, she may not like it. On the other hand, I saw something once that said that women in short skirts get more callbacks, if the interviewer is a man.

> **Journey 1990:** Agree with Amber on the skirt length. Cover knees. Nothing above the knee.

> **Cameron 1980:** Navy or grey is better choice for suit. Or a dress with a jacket. I would say the skirt should not be

long. Below the knee is too dowdy! But not too short - certainly no shorter than mid-thigh. On the shoes, wear plain pumps in a conservative color (black or brown).

Journey 1990: I would not wear high spike heels. Low block heels.

Cameron 1980: Just don't wear those dowdy low block heels. Spike heel pumps are best.

Amber 1985: Wear comfortable shoes! No high spikes! But if you are short, the higher, the better. Taller girls get more job offers. Short girls are not taken seriously in law firms.

Journey 1990: Wing tip oxfords would be a good choice.

Cameron 1980: I would stay away from those wing tip shoes, which are distracting.

Chris 1975: I think whatever you wear is going to be fine. If you've gotten this far, your credentials are obviously great and that is what they are looking at! I would focus on practicing some answers to the standard questions, get a good night's sleep and then just go in there and knock 'em dead!!

As the above thread demonstrates, advice on an internet forum can be sharply conflicting. There is no obvious way to reconcile the radically divergent views Autumn1998 received. Further, there is no easy way for Autumn to tell which advice she should follow, having received diametrically opposite views on a number of points. The only uncontradicted (and perhaps the soundest) advice she got was from Chris1975: to focus more on what she is going to say than what she is going to wear.

Autumn sought advice about a relatively discrete matter — what to wear for a job interview. The question was a reasonable one, and some of the answers she got were reasonable as well. Following any of the sartorial advice would not have negatively affected the outcome of Autumn's interview. However, Autumn's comfort and confidence in how she presents herself are critically important in the interview, and there is a risk that some of the posts caused Autumn to have doubts and anxiety.

Crowdsourced mentoring can be fun and interesting, but no one should make any significant career decision on the basis of a nameless, faceless, poster on an internet forum. Message boards and internet forums sometimes simply create confusion and doubt. Autumn came to the message board seeking guidance on an issue that, while it might not make or break her career, is important to her right now. Sharing your experiences and soliciting advice and opinions is a great way to gather information, but *you* must be the sole arbiter of the validity of the advice.

3.6 Be careful about taking advice

You need to be careful about taking advice. Not only do you need to be careful from whom you take advice, but you have to be aware that sometimes even good people give bad advice. It's as important to recognize and not follow bad advice as it is to recognize and follow good advice.

Bad advice can be dangerous, sometimes irreparably so. We have all read stories about people that have been put through months of costly and painful medical treatment because their doctors thought they had a serious disease, only to later discover that they were not sick at all, or had a totally different ailment which was being made worse by the treatment. Just as you need to be careful about which health care professionals you listen to, you need to be careful about whom you take career advice from.

How can you tell when the advice you are hearing is bad? There are five signs that you should always look for. If at least four of the five signs are present, the advice is almost certainly bad and you should not follow it. If three of the five signs are present, the advice may be bad, and you need to get more information or at least evaluate the advice with extra care before following it.

Here are the five signs of bad advice:

    1. The advice is illogical or irrational on its face. Examples of this are: advice to quit a job when you don't yet have a new one.

2. *The advice is generic or commonplace. Stated differently, the advice is found on the Internet on numerous sites, or consists of a popular expression, cliché or platitude. For example: advice to "stay in your lane."*
3. *Family members (your siblings, parents, or spouse) all disagree with the advice.*
4. *Your gut tells you not to do it. If your intuition and instincts are telling you not to follow the advice, you need to listen to yourself and ignore the advice.*
5. *Taking the advice would mean foreclosing another option or avenue that is extremely important to you professionally or personally.*

How can you tell if advice is good and you should follow it? There are three signs that you are getting good advice:

Good advice feels immediately liberating.

Advice should free you to take action, not shut you down. Receiving sound, truthful advice will make you feel energized and eager to begin acting upon it. On the other hand, if the advice makes you feel constrained or inhibited, it might not be the best advice.

As a general rule, advice to speak up and tell the truth about something that is important is better than advice to keep quiet or to hide important information. The former is liberating, the latter constraining.

Good advice is specific to you and your situation.

Advice that is given broadly to an entire group of people is often worthless. It might not apply to all or to any specific individual. Advice that is directed to you *specifically* is worthy of consideration, as opposed to generic advice given to a group in which you are a member. An example is advice given broadly to everyone in your situation, generation, or demographic group. Such advice might have some relevance, but is more likely to lack any real merit.

Good advice is recognized by your intuition.

If, upon hearing advice, you feel internal resistance, and that feeling persists, this is usually a sign that there is something wrong with the advice, at least as it pertains to you. The resistance that you feel when hearing certain advice might actually be your intuition warning you that the advice is bad.

Some popular self-help books suggest that internal resistance to a recommended course of action is a flaw in the person hearing the recommendation, not a flaw in the recommendation. This is as far from the truth as it can be. Resistance is not something to ignore or override; resistance comes from intuition.

Malcolm Gladwell, in his groundbreaking book, *Blink*, wrote about the reliability of intuition over a conscious thought process. Intuition is not emotion or whimsy, but is the unconscious processing of a lifetime of information to produce an instantaneous conclusion. Intuition is like a personal logic chip — a human microprocessor.

Intuition is a greatly misunderstood power. In evaluating advice, there is no superior tool than intuition.

3.7 Sometimes, go backward

A relationship with a mentor may be exhilarating at first, but after a while, you may feel that you are moving backward. A mentor may even tell you to do things that seem backward. He may suggest that you give up what you are doing and start over in a new field or specialty, take a job that involves a pay cut, or quit your job and go back to school. If you don't have absolute confidence in your mentor and his judgement, such suggestions will seem ridiculous.

What may appear backwards, in fact may not be. Sometimes a step back is actually progress. While "fast-forward into the present" may sound smart in a simplistic way, it's often not the best way forward. Not everyone operates well with the newest level of technology, the newest season's fashions, or the newest model car. It may be better, cheaper, and faster to have an earlier operating system or an older car. The future looks to the past for inspiration; the newest does not always mean the best. The same is true for one's current station in life — what you are doing now is not always the path to success. A mentor may see that a protégé needs to get off his current path in order to move forward in his life and career.

3.8 How a mentor operates

A protégé wants a mentor to be a positive influence on his career, if not in other aspects of his life. The scope of a mentor's positive influence, and the precise way in which a mentor exerts that influence, will depend on the protégé's individual relationship with the mentor.

A completely committed mentor will take an all-encompassing view of his protégé. Such a mentor can touch the way a protégé organizes his life, from the structure of his education and experience to the arrangement of his lifestyle and career.

Advice-giving is one avenue of a mentor's influence, but it is not the only one. A protégé might also be influenced by the mentor's lifestyle. If the mentor lives without technology, the protégé will experience face-to face-interactions with him unfiltered by a smartphone. If the mentor is a vegan who eats only organic food, the food the protégé eats with him becomes part of the experience — part of the mentor's stamp. Eating with a mentor at the mentor's favorite restaurant can be part of experiencing what the mentor's world is like, but eating at the protégé's favorite place is part of the mentor's role in understanding his protégé.

If the mentor smokes, drinks, or gambles, the protégé's experience will be affected by this as well. While not every protégé will share in these activities, a mentor's habits, both good and bad, can make a mark on the mentor–protégé experience. A protégé is not made in the image of his mentor but will become an echo of his mentor's dispositions.

A protégé should not idolize a mentor too much, because that might impair the protégé's objectivity. Objectivity is necessary especially when a mentor is or becomes personally flawed, or is no longer adequate as a mentor.

A protégé may be also guided by how the mentor operates. Watching a mentor work is the most typical way that this occurs. For example, an artist may walk through the creation of a painting or sculpture with an art mentor. A journalist may work with a writing mentor on a book project. A musician may accompany his music mentor to busk in the NYC subway or for a recording session.

3.9 Doubt or certitude

One of the biggest impediments to progress in one's career is doubt. Should I go to law school or medical school? Should I go to School A or School B? Should I pursue the private sector or public service? Should I leave Firm ABC and go to Firm XYZ? There are hundreds of questions that confront a person in his lifetime, but only about half a dozen questions will make or break the course of a career.

The *New Advent Catholic Encyclopedia* describes "doubt" as:

> A state in which the mind is suspended between two contradictory propositions and unable to assent to either of them. . . . Doubt is opposed to *certitude*, or the adhesion of the mind to a proposition without misgiving as to its truth[;] certitude may be produced either by reason (which deals with evidence) or by faith (which rests on authority).

It is impossible to gain certitude as to questions about what direction to take, or what decision to make, by reason alone. Definitive evidence about the future is simply unavailable. Resolving such questions always involves a leap of faith.

When you are in doubt, a mentor may give you bold, even outrageous, advice. If you trust your mentor completely, you will follow your mentor's advice, no matter how scary it may seem. You will have certitude by faith.

PART 4

Types of Mentors

PART 4:

Types of Mentors

4.1 Bold mentors

Just because a mentor tells you to do something, does not necessarily mean that it's right. Chances are, however, that if you have the right mentor, the advice — however shocking it is — will be right, but perhaps not for the reasons you think.

Rayne, a young lawyer, was struggling with a judge. Every time she appeared before Judge Burke, no matter how prepared she was or what she said or did, the Judge berated her. If he asked her a question and she did not have the answer, he would make gratuitous, insulting comments, like "You don't know much, do you?" or "Are you ever going to come in here with better arguments?" He interrupted her frequently, and seemed to challenge every word she said. If she apologized, he berated her for apologizing. He did this several times in front of clients.

She was a senior associate aspiring to partnership in her law firm. Any kind of potential negative feedback threatened her prospects of becoming a partner. From her perspective, the situation with Judge Burke was horrible and needed to stop.

Rayne called Judge McGann, the judge she had clerked for several years before and whom she regarded as a mentor. Judge McGann knew Judge Burke very well. Rayne hoped to get some insight and good advice.

After Rayne had explained what was happening and relayed some of Judge Burke's comments, Judge McGann told her: "I have no idea why Peter is treating you this way. Here's what I suggest. Call his chambers and ask to speak to him. Tell his secretary who you are and that you are not calling about a pending matter. When he takes your call, tell him you have noticed that whenever you appear before him, he appears displeased with you, and that you want to know what you are doing wrong and what you can do to improve the situation."

The advice given to Rayne by her mentor was controversial, if not outrageous. Few lawyers would actually call up a judge and confront him about his courtroom demeanor. Most lawyers, in fact, would view approaching a judge in this manner as extremely ill-advised. However, Rayne trusted Judge McGann, whom she regarded as her mentor. She made the call to Judge Burke, following the script suggested by Judge McGann.

Judge Burke — as Judge McGann predicted — took the call. After Rayne had said what she had to say and asked her question, Judge Burke said, "Rayne, I am not displeased with you at all. There is absolutely nothing you are doing wrong. In fact, you are coming to court consistently prepared and doing a great job for your clients. I simply like to give all new lawyers appearing before me a hard time."

After the phone call, every time Rayne appeared before Judge Burke, he was extraordinarily respectful to her. His good judicial temperament when Rayne appeared before him was remarkable, since he was not generally this way with other lawyers. Clients and other counsel noted that Rayne had great rapport with Judge Burke, more so than any of the other lawyers who appeared before him.

Rayne wondered why in the world Judge McGann had given her that advice, and why she had followed it — advice which, in retrospect, seemed outrageous. Calling a judge to discuss his behavior could have turned out very badly. There could have been severe consequences if Judge Burke had responded differently. Possibly, Judge McGann did not send Rayne on this course of action blindly. Knowing Judge Burke well, Judge McGann may have known that

Judge Burke would not retaliate against Rayne and that he would respond constructively. Judge McGann may even have called Judge Burke in advance and discussed the call, and he may have asked Judge Burke to be kind to his former clerk. Rayne realized that she was fortunate and that the advice from anyone other than Judge McGann might have been disastrous.

Reflecting on this many years after, Rayne also realized that for her to call Judge Burke and ask him directly what she was doing wrong did much more than merely improve her experience before that court. The very act of doing this emboldened Rayne in every way. Having directly confronted a federal judge about his behavior, she was not easily scared or deterred. Whenever anyone berated, belittled, or criticized her, it no longer affected her the way it used to. She recognized that sometimes such behavior may be artificial. She learned to evaluate criticism dispassionately and objectively. Moreover, from that point forward, she had far less hesitation in calling anyone out, or in asking anyone for anything.

Judge McGann, in his wisdom and knowing and caring about Rayne as he did, knew that she would take his advice, and he was not going to send Rayne on a disaster mission. He also knew the experience would embolden and transform her.

4.2 Gender blind mentors

A recent study on gender and racial bias in the legal profession found that women in law and business are expected to act "like women." If women defy gender stereotypes, there are consequences. Corporations and law firms have implicit codes of behavior expected of women, and they can be very different from the behavior that is expected of, or tolerated from, men.

Alexa, a lawyer, was often the only woman in a settlement conference. Her client, the opposing counsel, and the opposing parties were almost always men. They would reach a point in a meeting where the discussion would get heated, and the men would call for a bathroom break. Everyone would head to the men's room, including her client, while continuing to discuss the settlement. She would be left behind. When the men returned, the settlement discussion would have gone several steps forward, without her input or advice to her client. Essentially, she was being rendered ineffective because she could not go into the men's room. This had recently happened in a major case where the negotiations shifted in a manner that her client considered unfavorable, all during the men's room break.

Alexa often confided in Kathryn, a woman at her church. Kathryn was a theology student and often had an unusual way of looking at things. Alexa told Kathryn about the situation. Kathryn said, "That's completely unacceptable. The next time this happens and the men all head to the men's room, including your client, you just go and follow them in there."

At first, Alexa wasn't sure if Kathryn was serious or not. The advice was controversial, perhaps even transgressive. Alexa decided she would never actually do this.

About a month later, Alexa was in another all-male settlement conference. The negotiations became very heated. About an hour and a half into the meeting, one of the men called for a bathroom break. They all got up and headed to the men's room — Alexa's client included — while continuing to talk about the settlement. Alexa remembered what Kathryn had said. Alexa got up and followed the men heading toward the men's room. When the group entered the men's room, Alexa followed them in.

Once everyone was in the men's room — Alexa included — the men all froze. One of them asked her, "What are you doing in here?" She said, "You're discussing the settlement, and I need to be part of that discussion."

News of the incident spread fast. As is typical in Manhattan, what happened downtown in mid-morning made its way to midtown by lunchtime.

Interestingly, no one ever tried the "men's room move" on Alexa again. At future meetings, the opposing counsel and opposing client would always wait until Alexa's client was out of the men's room before going in.

Alexa certainly did not act like a woman is expected to act in this situation. Kathryn viewed Alexa independent of her gender, and advised Alexa to break gender role expectations. Kathryn's advice caused Alexa dissonance when she first heard it. In fact, Alexa didn't expect to actually follow the advice, but when finding herself in the situation again, Kathryn's words resonated in her head. Kathryn's advice was pivotal for Alexa.

Alexa eventually became highly regarded as a strong, powerful negotiator who always obtained highly favorable outcomes for her clients.

Would a male mentor have given the same advice to Alexa, or was Kathryn in a unique position to give the advice because she was a woman?

A mentor does not need to be the same sex, gender, race, ethnicity, religion, or sexual orientation as you. But a mentor has to see you independently of any of those characteristics.

4.3 Sponsor mentors

Protégés often need both a mentor and a sponsor. Sometimes the most effective sponsor is, in fact, a mentor, but it may be one who is not an obvious choice as a sponsor.

Jamie, a first-year litigation associate at an Am Law 100 firm, was worried. She felt she wasn't catching on to anything that she was expected to do. She wasn't getting much encouragement from the partners she was working for. Some of them implied that she wasn't aggressive enough, didn't write well enough, and didn't have an instinct for strategy.

One partner, Daniel, told Jamie that she simply didn't "have the DNA to be a litigator." That comment was the last straw. She was afraid her job might be in jeopardy.

She was at a loss over what she was doing wrong or how to get on the right path. Out of frustration and concern with the criticism she was getting, Jamie sought the advice of Kara, a senior litigation associate in her firm. She didn't know Kara well, but she looked up to her. Jamie admired Kara's overall personality, particularly what Jamie perceived as equanimity. She admired the way Kara was always put-together and polished, without overdoing it. Kara was always prepared and ready for the unexpected conference call or meeting, but she didn't always have on fresh lipstick or wear heels. Often, she would be wearing flats or her hair tied back, particularly if she was working late. Her looks were secondary to her mission; her style was there to serve her job, not vice versa.

Jamie saw Kara as someone confident and comfortable in her own skin. The office "buzz" was that Kara was a shoo-in to be promoted to partner. Jamie could tell that although Kara was a bit on edge about the looming partnership decision, she did her best to keep her anxiety under wraps.

Jamie told Kara the feedback she was getting from the partners — including Daniel's "DNA" comment — and expressed her confusion and frustration. Jamie asked Kara point blank: "What can I do to improve my work?"

Kara listened to Jamie very carefully. She liked Jamie. She liked that Jamie had serious academic credentials and worked hard. While Kara had not worked with Jamie, Kendra, another partner who had worked with Jamie, told Kara that Jamie was "whip-smart" and a quick study. Kara's general impression of Daniel, the male partner who made the "DNA" comment, was that he may not have been taking Jamie as seriously as she deserved to be taken. Kara was reluctant to label it implicit bias, but she felt there might just be a touch of that.

She was pleased that Jamie sought her out for advice and wanted to help her. She knew that a junior associate faced a lot of challenges to advancement at a large firm. She also knew there were many unwritten rules and obstacles that were daunting even for the most brilliant associate.

Kara thought very carefully about what Jamie said and how to respond. She knew instinctively not to lay it all on Jamie at once. She didn't want Jamie to feel overwhelmed by giving her too much information. She decided to give Jamie a couple of tips at a time, and let her have space to work on them at her own pace.

After a few moments of silence, Kara said: "Jamie, everyone has trouble at the beginning. There's nothing wrong with you. I think Daniel sometimes has a hard time seeing, as a lawyer, anyone that doesn't fit his image of a lawyer. The world is full of people like that — you just have to ignore it and power through. Eventually he'll come around." Jamie responded, "I hope so. I guess I have to put his comment out of my head." Kara said, "Yes. If you don't, it will just make you nuts. In the meantime, I'm not saying that your writing is bad, but everyone can improve. There is a CLE class that I have been to a couple of times on writing skills for lawyers that makes a huge difference. It's only a couple of hours, and it's fun, too. I'll send you the link."

Jamie left Kara's office feeling hopeful. She followed Kara's advice, and, a few weeks later, went back to Kara to talk to her about some research she was assigned. The partner wanted an oral report before a written memo. Kara gave Jamie a couple of tips about how she should present the findings to the partner. Kara had Jamie rehearse the presentation and gave her some suggestions to sharpen it.

Jamie started to seek out Kara for other advice, as well, such as what to wear to court or a meeting where she was accompanying partners. From time to time, Kara would stop by Jamie's office and offer a tidbit of information about opportunities for associates and her impression of whether they would be worthwhile for Jamie or a total waste of time.

Gradually, Jamie found that the partners who had been so critical of her at first were now saying that she was doing a great job. She was getting more and more assignments from them as well, which was a positive sign.

The following year, as Jamie was starting her third year at the firm, Kara was promoted to partner. The firm launched a mentor program where associates who had been at the firm at least two years could request a partner as a mentor. Jamie requested Kara. When Kara heard about this, she went to Jamie's office and told her she would be delighted to be her mentor, but was surprised Jamie had requested her. Kara said, "I'm just a first-year partner. I don't have much power at all. I just assumed you would want someone more senior who could be more influential as a sponsor." Jamie said, "You have no idea how much you've helped me already. You've been my mentor all along, even before it was official."

Kara did not see herself as a powerful sponsor, but in fact she was. Kara enlisted Jamie to work with her on all of her cases, and Jamie became one of the "go-to" associates for the partners in Kara's group.

Eventually, Kara's group was recruited by another, larger firm. The group wanted to bring one or two associates, and Kara recommended that Jamie be offered the chance to go with them. When the group left — Kara and Jamie included — the new firm provided a larger platform, the practice grew, and Jamie's career thrived. In time, she became a partner.

Jamie credits Kara with being not only her mentor, but her sponsor as well. Sponsorship was not something that Jamie was consciously looking for or expecting from Kara, but it was something that Kara seamlessly provided.

4.4 Cold, distant or dissolute mentors

Not every mentor is a warm, all-around good citizen like Kara. Some mentors are cold and distant. Some mentors are abrasive or eccentric. Some mentors are dissolute and have addictions, such as food, alcohol, drugs, sex or gambling.

The choice of a mentor is a complex one. Sometimes the best mentor is one with flaws. Getting the most from a flawed mentor can be a challenge at first, but can be easier once you know how to manage him.

Every time Jasper, a lawyer, talked to his mentor Emmett, Emmett would say to him, "Don't screw up" or "Try not to do something cosmically stupid." Emmett's comments had a demeaning edge, as if he thought Jasper would do something stupid unless Emmett specifically told him not to. Despite Emmett's propensity to insult him, Jasper found that Emmett often had unique, groundbreaking advice about legal strategy or business development that Jasper could use.

Sometimes when Andy visited his mentor Joe, Joe would have had a couple of drinks at lunch and not process what Andy was saying. Sometimes while under the influence, Joe could become mean or hostile. While Andy found this annoying, when Joe was sober, he was inspiring, funny, and helpful.

Often when Steve would visit his mentor Wayne, Wayne would be silent and expressionless for what seemed like an eternity. When Steve asked Wayne a question, it might be a full minute before Wayne said anything. Sometimes, Wayne just stared at Steve and had nothing to say. This approach was disconcerting, to say the least. When Wayne did say something, however, he was always right. Wayne had a clarity about situations that was truly refreshing.

Here are some tips for dealing with a cold, distant, or dissolute mentor.

1. Treat him like a normal person, even when he is not. This can be a challenge. Resist the temptation to respond to coldness, hostility, or cutting comments, with coldness, hostility, or cutting comments. Be authentic. Don't put up a front or distance yourself while in the conversation. This simple technique can elevate the level of any conversation.

2. Be direct — even blunt — when you have to be. Every time Emmett told Jasper "don't be stupid" or "don't screw up," Jasper responded, "That gives me no information."

3. Just because a person is cold and uncommunicative doesn't mean he likes it when others are cold and uncommunicative to him. When Wayne responds to a conversation with a long silence, Steve asked him a direct question, such as, "What do you think?" and gave Wayne time to respond. If Wayne responded in a terse or brusque fashion, Steve focused on content only. Steve always responded only to the content of what Wayne said, not his tone or manner.

4. Know when not to ask his advice. Andy learned not to visit Joe after lunch, and to simply leave when Joe was not completely focused. If Joe became abusive, Andy would tell him, "Call me when you are in a position to talk." If Andy got a drunken text from Joe, he deleted it.

5. Don't take his communications (or lack thereof) personally.

4.5 Truth-telling mentors

A protégé can't be constantly fact checking his mentor. He needs to be able to believe what his mentor tells him. Only a fully truth-telling mentor will be trusted when he tells his protégé something shocking or radical.

Years ago, Tim, a business colleague, recounted a personal experience that he had while he was struggling in business, as well as with an addiction. Tim was walking along the beach when suddenly there was an older man walking next to him. He started a conversation with the man and explained that he had taken a vacation by himself to find direction in his life. Tim told the man that he was struggling with the dilemma of telling the truth when doing so would have severely negative consequences, and might even subject him to criminal prosecution and incarceration. The older man said, "A man who always tells the truth is always believed. A man who lies once is never believed." The man then suddenly vanished.

Tim may have been under the influence of a substance at the time. However, it doesn't take a hallucination to recognize the importance of truth.

A mentor needs to tell the truth. Not the truth as he sees it, but the actual truth. This is not as easy as it sounds.

4.6 Personally bonded mentors

While an in-law or other family member may be an unusual mentor, he may sometimes be an ideal one, particularly if you have been stuck for a long time. A good mentor is one who knows you well enough to see your blind spots and to set you on a path to clarity. Probably no one knows your blind spots more than an in-law.

Blake was in a rut. Her career was ostensibly successful, but she constantly struggled with getting to the next level. In her early 40s, she was an associate general counsel in a "too big to fail" bank. She had plateaued in the job. There was little prospect that she would be promoted to deputy general counsel, much less to general counsel. She made far less money than her counterparts in private practice, although she knew how risky their positions could be and how much they struggled with pressures to bring in business, something that she did not have to do.

She didn't know how to move forward. Even worse, she didn't know who to turn to. Her mentor in the bank had left, and, while at the bank, he had never progressed beyond a mid-level post. She wasn't sure he would have the perspective she was looking for.

It was the dead of summer, and Blake and her husband, Ryan, were going on vacation with Ryan's parents. There was nothing she could do at the moment except to put her career crisis out of her mind for the time being.

Ryan's parents, Michael and Molly, had a house in Oak Bluffs on Martha's Vineyard where they would spend the summer. Every July, Blake and Ryan spent a couple of weeks with them. Ryan and his mother loved to go to the beach every morning. Blake and Ryan's father preferred to spend the day walking around the island. One day when Ryan and Molly were at the beach, Blake and Michael took a long walk and ended up at a favorite seafood restaurant.

Michael was a retired lawyer, formerly deputy general counsel at a large aircraft manufacturer. Blake had never talked to her in-laws about struggles in her law career. She didn't want to burden them or cause them to worry about her and Ryan. However, on this particular day, Michael asked her how things were going at the bank and whether she saw herself staying there. She decided to share with him that she was feeling stuck and didn't know what to do.

Michael said, "I've sensed this coming for at least the past three or four years. I didn't see you getting promoted given the politics of the bank. I didn't sense you were all that happy staying in your present position permanently. Also, with reports of layoffs every couple of years, you must be worried about your job security. I was wondering what you were going to do, but it wasn't my place to ask." Blake had no idea it was that obvious. She asked, "What should I do?"

Michael showed her a picture on his phone he had taken of a sign outside a local store. The sign read, "What would you do if you knew you could not fail?"

Blake found the idea of looking for a new position to be overwhelming. She did not even know what she wanted to do. Michael suggested she start by talking to and networking with her counterparts at other banks.

When vacation was over, Blake started talking with her contacts. She quickly found that either they were miserable and worried about their own jobs or that there were no slots that they knew of — or both. She went back to Michael for advice. He gave her a simple tip. Picture the specific job or type of job you want. Picture where it is, what you would be doing, and who you will be working with. Then find "six degrees of separation" from that job: who is in charge of hiring for that position, who knows them, and who you know that may be able to make a connection. Start talking to people. He said,

"You can't just sit in your office, eat at your desk every day, and then at the end of the day go home. You have to give up personal time and put out some real energy to do this."

Blake was a bit taken aback. She never realized that Michael perceived her as unenergetic. She dreaded starting over and trying to make new contacts. She found this daunting.

She told Michael that she didn't know where to start. He said, "You don't have to know. Start anywhere. Start everywhere. Talk to the person next to you on a plane or in a store. Talk to people you meet at events. Find out what they do and where they work. Have lunch with old friends from law school or the bank. Before you know it, you will have contacts that may lead, directly or indirectly, to a new position."

Blake wasn't sure she could do this, or that it would actually work. But she didn't want to admit to her father-in-law that she hadn't taken his advice or that she had made no progress. She set out to make connections, at least one a day.

In her second week of making contacts, she had lunch with an old law school friend, Joyce. Joyce was in the U.S. Attorney's office. Joyce's husband, Stan, was a partner in a law firm. Blake told Joyce what was on her mind and how she felt a job in private practice was out of her reach because she could not assure portable business. Joyce was sympathetic but offered no advice or suggestions.

A week later, Blake got a call from Joyce. Joyce said, "Stan and I were driving to our daughter's soccer game, and I was telling him about our lunch last week. When he heard you were looking to leave the bank, he almost stopped the car. He said, 'Are you serious? Blake wants to leave the bank? Roger, our senior partner in charge of the financial institutions practice, is super busy and has been looking to hire someone with in-house bank experience.' Are you interested in talking to Roger?" Blake knew Roger and would jump at the chance to work for him. At Joyce's urging, Blake sent Roger a letter and resume that afternoon. In a month, she had a job offer in hand and was leaving her position at the bank.

At Roger's firm, Blake grew in the job, working now as outside counsel to the bank she had left, as well as other clients. She was eventually promoted to partner.

Blake credits Michael with understanding her well enough to have recognized both her dissatisfaction and inertia, which someone outside her family might not have seen. As her father-in-law, Michael had special insight into her personality, and was able to give strong, solid advice that was right for her. Without his guidance, she might have ended up stuck or on the wrong path.

4.7 Transient mentors

Not all mentors need to be long term. A transient mentor serves the role of a mentor but his role may not be ongoing. Transient mentors are real mentors, they are just short term.

Kelly felt her career was at an impasse. A mid-level partner at a large law firm, she had built her practice reasonably well, but she was not at the income level that some of her more successful partners were. She was well known, but she was not a household word. She did not have a Wikipedia page.

Kelly had not seen her former mentor, Justin, in five years, but today, she wanted to talk to him. She wasn't exactly sure what she wanted to talk to him about or what she would ask him exactly, but she wanted to talk to him.

When Kelly tried to call Justin, she found his phone disconnected. She looked for his contact information on his firm's website, but he wasn't listed anymore. She called someone else in his firm and learned that he had retired and moved to Florida.

Kelly really needed a mentor, and hers had moved to Florida without giving her his cell phone number.

She was busy and didn't have time to hunt Justin down. She had been pulled into a large securities case that soon would be going to trial, in which her firm served as local counsel for a prominent trial lawyer at another firm, Eric. Kelly also found herself planning an awards dinner at which Marc, a prominent litigation partner in her firm, was being honored. Finally, her firm had just merged with a West Coast firm headed by a celebrity litigator, Richard. In the midst of these occurrences, Kelly realized that these three men who had suddenly appeared in her life — Eric, Richard, and Marc —

were all Justin's age. She started looking at each of them as a possible replacement mentor for Justin.

She intended to approach Eric first, but after the securities trial they worked on ended, she wasn't able to connect with him for lunch right away. As time passed, Kelly didn't bother to try to have lunch with Eric, perhaps because spending so much time with him during the trial had lessened her enthusiasm about seeing him.

At the awards dinner, she did, however, have a chance to spend time with Marc, as she was sitting next to him at the firm's table. Marc was an icon of the LGBTQ community and was being honored for his work on a number of landmark Supreme Court cases. For decades, Marc had been a quintessential mentor and role model for many. If anyone was a source of good advice, it was Marc. Over dinner, she asked him about his career and for advice about her own. He told her that people like the two of them chose their own path. He told her that if she kept practicing in the area of law she loved and was known for, her career would keep advancing. This was encouraging and hopeful, but she still had unanswered questions.

Finally, Richard was visiting the New York office for a week. She got his schedule, hoping to drop by his office during his stay. His schedule, however, proved so hectic that she had difficulty catching him. The third time she went to his office, she learned that he had just left and was headed to a meeting a few blocks away. Kelly decided to try to meet him, and perhaps get on his calendar for a visit later.

She raced down the hall toward the elevator, but just missed him. She took another elevator, hoping to catch Richard in the lobby. When she got downstairs, there was no one there. Thinking she had missed him, she paused, wondering if she should try to find him on the street. She felt like a stalker. Just then, another elevator car opened, and Richard emerged. Kelly walked over to him and introduced herself. He seemed nonplussed at being approached this way, but smiled and shook her hand. She told him that she had been trying to meet him and asked if she could walk with him as he headed to his meeting. "Yes, of course," said Richard.

As they walked and talked, Kelly got right to the point. "I'm 55 years old." He replied, "Well, I'm a lot older than you." For a split second, it felt as if she were making some sort of awkward sexual advance. She laughed and said, "Yes, I know how old you are, that's why I wanted to talk to you. I want your advice. You have had a great career at the highest level, and it's still going strong. What is your secret? I want to do this too. I want to be at the top of my game and stay there for a long time." He said, "Oh, that's going to be easy. You won't have any trouble at all with this. There are a few things. You are probably already doing all of them but you need to simply continue. It's easy." Now he had her full attention: secrets of a highly successful career to follow.

"First, you have to keep doing actual legal work for clients, and it has to be work that is sought after. You can have other people help you, but don't hand everything off to a junior person. If a client has a 'bet the company' case, you are the one they want as the first chair at the trial, not some junior guy that hasn't tried a case before. Second, you have to maintain passion and energy for what you are doing. If your heart's not in it, you need to get out and do something else. Otherwise, your career will start declining. Third, you have to maintain your health. If you have your health, you have everything." Kelly listened carefully and said, "That is all, really?" Richard said, "There is one more thing. You need to be focused and pay attention to what's going on now and not be stuck in the past or focused on the future, but it's obvious that you *are* extremely focused." Richard arrived at his destination and their conversation was winding down. He said to Kelly, "I'm happy to continue the conversation later or whenever. Look, you're doing great. You are young and have years ahead of you. You're going to keep moving forward; there is no doubt."

Kelly held on to her conversations with Marc and Richard for a long time. She realized that she did not need to replace Justin. She needed only transient mentors, and Richard and Marc were precisely that.

4.8 Younger mentors

Sometimes the path to a mentor is unusual, but it is always intuitive.

A mentor does not have to be in your field or to be older than you to understand you and be a source of guidance.

Esme's career path seemed to be a dead end. Ten years out of law school, she had a contract associate position with a mid-size firm doing foreclosure work. There was a lot of sameness in what she was doing. Foreclosures were a formulaic process. Even when a foreclosure was contested, or when it was resolved with a loan modification which avoided a foreclosure, the cases were predictable. Esme had a large caseload which kept her occupied, but she found the work soul-destroying. Moreover, contract associates like her were treated like second class citizens. The other associates saw the contract associates as having lesser credentials. The partners viewed the contract associates as temporary workers having no future in the firm and thus unworthy of any investment of time and energy.

While Esme drew an adequate paycheck, she knew this position was not permanent — and did not want it to be. She was going nowhere.

In frustration, Esme decided that she would join a health club. She would work out every night until something happened. It seemed irrational — perhaps even magical thinking — but she was so desperate, she was willing to try anything.

One of the perks of her membership was two free sessions with a personal trainer. On her first night at the gym, she was greeted by her trainer, Carlisle. Carlisle looked extremely young. In fact, he was ten years younger than Esme. Carlisle went through a fitness questionnaire with Esme, and then started her on warm-ups.

Carlisle asked Esme what had led her to start working out. She wasn't expecting to bare her soul. But her lightheadedness from the warm-up, and the unexpected intimacy of giving a complete stranger her fitness goals, caused an uncharacteristic honesty. "I'm miserable in my job. I didn't go to law school to end up doing such crappy work. The opposing counsel I deal with are lazy and rude. When borrowers don't have counsel, it's even worse. Half the time they don't speak any language I can understand, and they don't know why I'm trying to throw them out of their house." Carlisle paused, and then said, "Wow." Esme apologized for sharing so much. Carlisle quickly assuaged her, saying, "Oh, no, I am glad you shared. I want to help. Really." Esme said, "I don't know how you can." Carlisle responded, "At least I can make sure you get a great workout."

Two days later, Esme had her second session with Carlisle. Carlisle didn't mention their prior conversation, but he started telling her a story of his own. "I played football in college. I was good. Great, actually. Usually college football leads nowhere, but I was very lucky. I had a chance to be in the NFL. I shocked everybody and walked away. Everyone thought I was crazy to walk away from the chance to make so much money. But I really didn't want it. I didn't like anything about it. I wanted to be a massage therapist, or maybe a yoga instructor." Esme sat up, startled by Carlisle's revelation. "You actually gave up a starting salary that was ten times what you are making now, because you didn't like the idea of playing professional football?" Carlisle responded, "It's not that I don't love football. I really do. But the lifestyle and everything surrounding professional football — I just didn't want any part of it." After a slight pause, Carlisle added, "The decision saved my life."

Esme filed Carlisle's story away in her mind, thinking that it was interesting and unusual. He was a great trainer. She saw an immediate improvement in how she felt after two training sessions so she decided to continue twice a week. From time to time, Carlisle told her more of his story, and she shared more of hers. Carlisle had found his current position on LinkedIn. He said he always looked at the online job postings, and applying was easy. Carlisle said it might take twenty emails to get one interview, and five interviews to get one job offer, but that the time spent waiting was strangely calming.

Esme from time to time had browsed online job postings but had never previously applied for any. That night, however, she went home and worked on her resume, resolving to respond to some job postings. Nevertheless, she wasn't expecting to get any interviews or to find anything that didn't involve a pay cut. She didn't think she could handle a pay cut.

Esme found that there were plenty of firms looking for mid-level associates, and most of them did not want to consider a candidate who was ten years out of school. A few smaller firms were more flexible, however, and she got some interviews. After a few months, she received an offer. It was less money, but there seemed to be more growth potential — even eventual partnership. She liked the people. She needed a change. She accepted the offer.

Sometimes, when Esme is asked, "Who is your mentor?" she says, "My trainer, Carlisle. He saved my life." Her co-workers assume Esme means that Carlisle made her healthier and more fit. In fact, she means that he got her out of a dead-end job.

4.9 Unexpected mentors

A true mentor does not always fit the protégé's vision of a mentor, but instead may be someone whose demographics are very different from the protégé's preconception. A mentor might not fit the protégé's image of a wise older man, but could be an unexpected person — perhaps even very close in age and circumstances to the protégé — and become the most sage advisor in challenging times.

This is particularly true when the challenge is of a personal or family nature. Disruptions, whether family, health, or relationship related, can pose unexpected obstacles in a career. It is easy to go off course due to personal distractions. A mentor who is close in age and circumstances to the protégé may be the best person to provide direction.

Breaking into freelance writing was much easier for Rohan than it is for most others. Among other things, his parents were established authors. As a child, his mother introduced him to the written word when he was barely able to speak. His playroom was one of his parents' numerous libraries. There were shelves full of books in every room in the house. Rohan grew up with the expectation that he would write, and write well. He was not just talented, but had been rigorously trained.

Rohan had academic credentials to match his literary upbringing. He also excelled as a writer early on. While still an undergraduate, his work was published in *The Columbia Review*.

One Sunday night, only a couple of weeks after Rohan's first article was published in Atlantic Monthly, Rohan's phone rang. It was Bill, one of Rohan's editors. Without so much as "hello," Bill blurted out, "Did you know?" Rohan responded, "Do I know what?" "Turn on the TV," said Bill. Rohan's mother had just announced on national television that she had committed plagiarism in some of her early works. Rohan's mother admitted her misgivings as a writer over this, and said she was concerned about the example she set for Rohan.

Rohan was shocked by his mother's revelation. It only occurred to him later that her statement that she was concerned about the example she set for Rohan might be construed as an admission that she showed him how to copy other people's work. His mother's admissions might bring his own journalistic integrity into question. Rohan's life was about to change — maybe even turned upside down. His mother's admitted plagiarism would become an inescapable talking point for the foreseeable future.

Rohan put it out of his mind that evening. The next day, he woke to messages and emails, all seeking comment on his mother's announcement. His first reaction was annoyance. His second was concern.

His mother's plagiarism was a distraction that would take the focus away from him at a critical time when he was just breaking into the literary world. He felt a bit guilty for feeling this way. He loved his mother, she had done so much for him, and he should not be making this about himself.

Rohan already felt resentment over what he perceived as embarrassment on the part of people around him. Even his partner, Emilio, seemed uncomfortable. Rohan didn't want to talk to Bill, Emilio, or anyone. At a time when he needed friends and family, it seemed suddenly that he could not turn to either.

Rohan felt that his life was coming apart at the seams. He wanted to hide in his apartment and not answer the phone.

When Siobhan's number came up on his caller ID, however, he answered. Siobhan had been the graduate assistant in one of his advanced writing courses in college. In his junior year, unsure of where he was going academically, he sought her out as a sounding board. While only three years older than Rohan, she always had a fresh perspective that he valued. On many occasions, she had pointed him in the right direction. It was Siobhan who had urged him to pursue a freelance writing career after graduation.

Siobhan, after earning her doctorate degree, was now teaching at one of the city's prestigious universities, and was also a freelance writer. On this Monday morning, she called Rohan to say she was thinking about him and hoped he was surviving the feeding frenzy that inevitably followed these types of public revelations. Rohan was glad she had called and asked if they could meet for coffee.

Later, over coffee, Rohan confessed to her that he was concerned what this would mean for him. "Is that selfish? This is my mom. I ought to care how she is right now, not be obsessing over how this impacts me." Siobhan, sympathetic and practical, said, "I understand first-hand how mercurial publishers can be. It's not unreasonable for you to be concerned. Let's cut right to the question: how do you think this is going to impact you?" Rohan said, "I'm afraid it will cause my career to go sideways or even backwards now. My mother's plagiarism will dominate the conversation, that is all anyone will want to talk to me about, and no one will be looking at me or my writing seriously." Siobhan said, "It may just seem that way today, because this is still fresh in the news cycle." Rohan said, "I am afraid it's going to have a long half-life. For months I am going to be continually asked: 'Did you know?' and various other questions about my mother. I don't want to answer these questions." Siobhan said, "You don't have to answer them." Then, she explained, "You have three options. First option is: you can ignore the buzz surrounding it, as if it were not there, and try to change the subject when people ask. Second option is: you can hide or lay low for a while. Go away, or just not answer the phone. Third option is: be proactive, come up with a script about the situation, and whenever you are asked, stick with the script. Bring the subject back to your own message, which is you and your writing." Siobhan paused, and then went on. "I think the third option is the best, and really the only option for you. Anything else is simply not you, and is not in your best interest, either." Rohan responded, "I don't know if I can do that — this is my family." Siobhan said, "The reason you need to do it is because it *is* your family."

What Siobhan was suggesting sounded hard. But Rohan's intuition told him it was the best thing to do, and perhaps for him, the only thing.

Rohan had never before this moment seen Siobhan as his mentor. She didn't fit his image of what his mentor should look like, which was an older, gay man who was a famous author or journalist. She was obviously not a gay man — she was a lesbian — and only slightly older than Rohan. She was not an established author, only a young college professor at the beginning of her career. On this day, however, when what seemed to be a crisis had presented itself, he realized that she was his true mentor. There was no one else he felt he could turn to for advice in his life and career who would understand him and offer clarity. She understood the complexity of his situation better than anyone else could, because she was close to his age and experience.

PART 5
Reference Tools

PART 5:

Reference Tools

5.1 Workbook #1

This workbook can help you identify potential mentors.

Areas in which I want advice:	Who understands me?	Who do I admire?	Who can I talk to?
Education			
Career			
Job			
Personal			
Health			
Fitness			
Interpersonal Relationships			
Housing			
Financial			
Other			

5.2 Questions to ask a mentor

The most effective way to maximize the benefits of a mentor is to ask the mentor questions. The questions can range from general to specific. Questions can produce direct answers and lead to incisive discussions.

Some protégés may find it useful to write down the questions and answers, as well as their own reactions and comments [Workbook #2].

Here are some open-ended questions to ask a mentor which are intended to lead to a broader discussion.

- Do you have any advice for me as to how to move ahead in my career?
- Should I ask for a raise in salary, and if so, how should I go about it?
- Do I need to go back to school?
- Should I try to launch my own business venture?
- What can I do to feel less stuck?
- Is there a skill, talent or quality that I have that I am underusing?
- Is there a book that you think I might benefit from reading?
- What should I do when faced with this crisis?

5.3 Workbook #2

This workbook can help you solicit advice from a mentor and analyze that advice.

Areas in which I want advice	Questions for mentor	Answers from mentor	Comments
Education			
Career			
Job			
Personal fitness			

5.4 Workbook #3 (example)

The following is an example of how Workbook #2 might be filled in.

Areas in which I want advice	Questions for mentor	Answers from mentor	Comments
Education	*Should I go back to school and get an MBA?*	*An MBA may not do anything for you.*	*This advice is a relief. I don't want to move or go back to school but felt that perhaps I should.*
Career	*Should I stay with the government or try to get a job in the private sector?*	*I think you will be frustrated if you stay in your present position and would benefit from looking at your options.*	*I am suffering from inertia and need to start looking for a new position. If I don't, eventually I'll be moving backwards.*
Job	*How do I get through each day when I am really burned out?*	*Take a vacation.*	*I haven't had a vacation in a long time.*

Areas in which I want advice	Questions for mentor	Answers from mentor	Comments
Personal fitness	*I feel like a mess. What should I do?*	*Baby steps. Take a walk every day. Move up to running a couple of times a week. You will feel the difference in no time.*	*This is something I could start doing while on vacation.*

5.5 Mentor report card

How do you evaluate whether your mentor is a "Mentor X"? This test can help you evaluate your mentor.

Rating scale:

  5: Yes, all the time.

  4: Yes, most of the time.

  3: Not always, but more often than not.

  2: Sometimes.

  1: Almost never.

  0: No, never

	Score 0–5
Does your mentor see and understand who you really are?	_____
Does your mentor tell you the truth?	_____
Has your mentor opened doors for you?	_____
Does your mentor give you advice?	_____
Is the advice good?	_____
Does your mentor reduce your fear and doubt?	_____
Does your mentor fuel your ambition?	_____
Does your mentor help you rise above greed?	_____
After talking with your mentor, do you feel hopeful and happy?	_____
Does your mentor communicate with you in a way that works for you (by text, message, email, call or visit)?	_____
Is your mentor accessible?	_____
Total	_____

Interpretation of score:

44–55:	You have a Mentor X.
39–43:	You have a good mentor, but there is room for improvement in your relationship.
23–38:	Your mentor may not be the best match for you.
0–22:	You don't have a mentor.

PART 6

Beyond the mentor

PART 6:

Beyond the mentor

6.1 Transformation of a mentor–protégé relationship

A mentor–protégé relationship rarely lasts an entire lifetime. The relationship might outlast the mentorship, and go on as a friendship, a partnership, or even a marriage, but no longer as mentor–protégé. Like a trip in the wilderness with guides, sometimes one leaves you off in a place, and another guide takes over.

There are signs that a mentor–protégé relationship is over and that the relationship has taken a different direction. The events that arise at the end of a mentorship can sometimes be disturbing or shocking, such as when a mentor crosses a personal boundary, becomes a rival, or engages in exploitative or unethical behavior. They are, however, the inevitable inflection points that signify that the mentorship has come to an end.

6.2 Boundaries

During her first month at one of the country's oldest and most highly regarded law schools, Grace identified Professor James as a potential mentor. At the end of her first year, she applied to become his research and teaching assistant, and was thrilled when he selected her.

As his assistant, she was able to spend an hour a week in his office, during which he would assign projects. She listened to his perspective on a wide range of subjects including the law, academia, and law firms. Before teaching, he had been a partner at a Wall Street firm. During on-campus recruiting, Professor James steered Grace to certain New York firms where he had contacts. His recommendation went a long way in securing her eventual offer to a top-drawer New York firm.

After graduation, they kept in touch. At least once a year, he would travel to New York on business, and they would always get together for dinner. She recalls vividly the dinner they had the year she hoped for a promotion to partner. His advice had been invaluable in the past, and she was looking for his guidance at this most difficult of career crossroads.

Halfway through the main course, he said something to her that was unlike anything he had ever said to her before. He said, "Is this all you want?" Confounded by the question, she said, "How do you mean?" He responded: "You're a single woman. Since moving to New York, you seem to be singularly focused on your career. You have no husband or children. Don't you want something more from your life?" So surprised was she by the question, Grace didn't know how to respond. She said nothing.

The following year, when Grace saw Professor James for their dinner during his annual trip to the city, she had good news: she had been promoted to partner. Perhaps due to the celebratory mood of the dinner, there were a few more drinks than usual. After the fourth glass of wine, Professor James moved very close to Grace and put his arm around her waist. She excused herself (ostensibly, to the ladies' room). When she returned, she said, "This has been lovely, but it's getting late. I have to be in the office early tomorrow — let's get the check."

When she got home, she struggled to process what happened. Although it was late, she called Kate, her best friend from law school. Kate's first reaction was "Professor James? Whoa — I did not see that coming. He'd be the last person I would expect that from." Grace confessed her shock, as well as her questioning of their prior relationship. Was she really a star student, worthy of being his teaching assistant and receiving his recommendation her to a top law firm, or were his actions driven by feelings of a different kind?

Kate, a successful lobbyist in Washington, D.C., reassured Grace that what happened over dinner was no reflection on Grace: "Trust me, this kind of thing happens all the time. In fact, it happens to everybody. While I am surprised that it was Professor James, I'm also surprised that you've not encountered this kind of thing before. In any event, what happened tonight has nothing to do with the past ten years, and takes nothing away from the fact of his being a great mentor."

The next morning, Grace woke up with a clearer vision of what had occurred the night before. A good night's sleep had dispelled her self-doubts. She was a most worthy protégé and talented lawyer in all respects; her performance at the firm, and her recent promotion, confirmed that. What happened the night before meant one thing, and one thing only: Grace and Professor James had both outgrown the mentor–protégé relationship. They could continue as friends and colleagues — or lovers, if they were both so inclined — but the mentorship was over.

Once a mentor crosses a boundary, it is a signal that the mentor–protégé relationship has ended.

6.3 Rivalry

Jasper had a number of job offers from law firms after his graduation from law school. He picked the firm with one of the country's leading experts in structured finance, for whom he would be working. He jumped at the chance to work with Emmett, despite Emmett's reputation for being cold, distant, and mercurial.

At the beginning, they got along very well. Jasper learned dozens of tricks of the trade. He learned what each client in the area wanted, both in legal representation and business referrals. He learned what terms were important and how to negotiate term sheets and transactional documents.

Having Jasper on his team proved so good for Emmett that his business doubled, as did his income. Recognizing Jasper's value, the firm enthusiastically promoted him to partner.

The firm held a surprise reception for Jasper to announce and celebrate his promotion. All the partners were there, including the managing partner of the firm. Well, not exactly all the partners: Emmett was absent. Later, Jasper learned Emmett was in his office, working on a document. Jasper chalked it up to one of Emmett's quirks.

As Jasper's first year as a partner went on, clients started to call Jasper directly to engage him for work. Many of these also referred new entrants into the finance area to Jasper. The business in the group was now three times what it had been when he started at the firm.

Right before compensation review, Jasper got a copy of his financial performance statistics. His numbers did not reflect any of the new clients or billings he had generated. When he inquired, he found out that Emmett had told the accounting department that Jasper should not have opened the matters, and instructed them to change the billing credit so it was reflected as Emmett's, not Jasper's.

Jasper also found out that Emmett, unbeknownst to Jasper, had called the new clients and told them that Jasper was "a bit in over his head" and that he, Emmett, would be taking over the matters.

While Jasper had looked to Emmett as a mentor for the past several years, Emmett now saw Jasper as a rival. Jasper realized that his relationship with Emmett had changed. Even if there was more he could learn from Emmett, professional rivalry had colored their relationship. Emmett was no longer Jasper's mentor.

But the story doesn't end there. Jasper approached Emmett, saying, "Look, we both stand to gain a lot by working together. Since the time we started working together, the business has tripled. But I simply can't continue to work this hard to bring work in, if I'm not getting any credit for it. Why don't we split credit 50-50 going forward?" Emmett responded, "Absolutely not. I'm the one the clients come here for. You're basically an elevated servant. The credit is all mine. End of conversation." Not deterred or angered by Emmett's crude rebuff, Jasper pressed on. He pointed out the numerous meetings he had where Emmett was not involved, and the increase in business since Jasper had become a partner. The message was clear: Jasper would not allow himself to be exploited, but he wanted to reach an agreement with Emmett so that they could continue to work together. Finally, Emmett relented and agreed to split the credit, with one-third to go to Jasper.

As things moved forward, Emmett found himself realizing how much Jasper was actually contributing, and eventually agreed to a 50–50 credit split with Jasper. The business continued to grow. More importantly, Emmett found himself enjoying practicing law more than ever before. Emmett's personal life changed, too. A long-time bachelor, he announced that he was getting married. A year later, Emmett decided to leave the law and move to Vancouver with his new wife, Rosalie.

At his going away party, Emmett said something that shocked everyone, especially Jasper. "When I first met Jasper, I was his mentor.

But after he became a partner, he became my mentor." There was laughter in the room. Emmett went on: "Jasper became my mentor in having a true partnership, something I had never really enjoyed before. At the beginning, I opened doors for him, but eventually, he opened doors for me."

The end of a mentor–protégé relationship because of rivalry does not mean the end of a relationship. Sometimes, it's simply the beginning of an entirely new relationship, as it was for Jasper and Emmett — and for Emmett and Rosalie.

6.4 Corruption

Jeffrey liked Chinese food. There was a Szechuan restaurant in Chinatown, South Palace, that Jeffrey loved. The Kung Pao chicken was his favorite.

Jeffrey's new associate, Alex, didn't like Chinese food. Alex was determined to find something on the South Palace menu that he liked. He discovered the broccoli chicken with light sauce. To make Jeffrey his mentor, there were going to be a lot of Szechuan lunches.

Alex knew exactly what he wanted from Jeffrey. Alex had come from the elite United States Attorneys' Office for the Southern District of New York. He was a star Assistant United States Attorney and had an outstanding track record of winning cases. He had joined the firm as senior associate for Jeffrey, the head of the firm's commercial disputes practice.

Trained by some of the country's best trial lawyers, there was nothing that anyone could really teach Alex about being in a courtroom. But there was a whole world of working with clients outside of the federal government that he had yet to experience, a world that was mystifying to him. To penetrate this world, he needed Jeffrey as a mentor.

Alex was fascinated by Jeffrey's panache and style, from his trademark dark blue bespoke suits to his limited-edition fountain pens. These signs of privilege seemed alluring to certain kinds of clients. Successful businessmen who were experiencing the effects of the recent economic downturn wanted a lawyer who was successful and who boldly displayed the external signs of success.

Most people meeting Jeffrey for the first time were surprised by his soft-spoken style, but were also quickly captivated by it. Watching Jeffrey in action in his quiet way, reeling in clients again and again, Alex learned that, when pitching a new client, a low-key, straightforward approach was the way to close the deal.

Once Jeffrey came back from a business trip and said he had met Robert, a well-known real estate developer, on the flight. Robert recognized Jeffrey from Jeffrey's picture on a magazine cover, touting him as New York City's top lawyer. By the time the flight landed, Jeffrey landed a new client too.

Robert had numerous personal guarantees on bank loans financing his real estate empire. The commercial real estate market was crashing, and the banks were threatening personal lawsuits against Robert on his guarantees. Robert found himself scrambling to protect his real estate empire, as well as his personal wealth. He turned to Jeffrey for advice.

Jeffrey came up with an ingenious plan.

Robert would invest in a new venture with David, the owner of South Palace. The new company — a restaurant chain named Palace Too — would be created as an offshore entity. Robert's ownership interests would be held indirectly through a complex structure. Robert's capital contribution would be virtually all his liquid assets, and he would also invest cash generated by his real estate operations. This structure would, presumably, render Robert's personal assets harder to reach by creditors who obtained judgments against him.

When Alex heard the plan, he questioned if it would work. While the transaction was not illegal, it might be challenged later as fraudulent. The firm might ultimately be tarnished by having set up the structure. Jeffrey said, "We can take that risk. Robert is paying the firm a $2 million retainer this week. This is just for his personal interests; we will get millions more as litigation counsel for his vast business empire. I'm the largest business producer in the firm; if other partners don't like it, they can leave."

Alex wanted to survive, to get clients, to become famous. But this wasn't the way he wanted to do it. He didn't want to be sheltering assets for any client who was willing to pay enough for it.

Jeffrey was offering to open doors for Alex that Alex didn't want to walk through.

Alex realized that he had gotten everything he could from Jeffrey as a mentor. He respected Jeffrey and would remain his associate, but Alex's relationship with Jeffrey as a mentor was over.

When a mentor leads you in a direction that is not right for you, it's a sign that the mentorship is over. He may continue to be your boss, colleague, and friend, but he is no longer your mentor.

6.5 Interiorization

Samantha was gripped with panic. She just got a text from her lawyer. Everything had been reviewed and the due diligence was completed. The contract was ready to be signed. Until she signed, she could still walk away. Once she signed the contract, she would pass the point of no return.

As she walked down Sixth Avenue, she rummaged through her bag for her phone. She had not talked to George since he retired and moved to London. It was 10 pm London time. Was it too late to call? She searched her emails for his mobile number. On the fifth ring, he picked up. "George, it's Sam. I hope I didn't disturb you." George dispensed with the pleasantries: "Samantha, what's up?" Samantha got straight to the reason for her call. "I am about to sign a contract to buy a condo. It's a major piece of real estate, and I'm signing a mortgage. This is Manhattan — it's a big mortgage. Should I do this?" George said, "You need a place to live. You can't sleep in your brokerage account. What's the problem?" Samantha said, "It's fine if things keep going as they're going, but what if my practice dries up?" George said, "You mean, what are you going to do if there are suddenly no more mergers and acquisitions in this country? Is that the question?" George sounded impatient, but Samantha knew he wasn't; he was simply trying to help her think clearly. George continued: "Everyone has complete confidence in you except for one person — you. Why is that? Sign the damn contract."

Samantha hung up, took a breath, went back to her office and signed the contract. As always, George gave her good advice; it was a decision that, in the years that followed, she was extremely glad she made.

George had retired and moved on, but Samantha didn't feel that she had outgrown her relationship with him as a mentor. Every so often she felt she needed to talk to him and get his quick take on something. He didn't always answer the phone, but when he did, he was always spot on.

A few years later, Samantha was at a career crossroads. She had a corporate opportunity that was exciting, but it felt risky. She wanted to talk to George, but his voice mail wasn't working. She was not able to reach him.

She found herself asking, "What would George say?" She knew as soon as she asked the question that the corporate job was not the right opportunity for her.

She realized in that moment that she didn't need to call George for advice any longer. His work was done. George's mentorship of Samantha was complete.

6.6 Relinquishment

In the science fiction series, *Star Trek*, a species called the Trill live in symbiosis with another species, symbionts that cannot live independently but can survive only if implanted in a Trill's body. The symbionts live for hundreds of years and carry the memories and experience of their hosts. When the host Trill dies, the symbionts are surgically transplanted to another Trill. Through the symbiont, the new host acquires all the memories and experiences of all previous hosts. A Trill with a symbiont is called a "joined" Trill. A joined Trill, even a very young one, thus may have hundreds of years of experience via the symbiont.

In *Star Trek: Deep Space Nine*, Jadzia Dax, a joined Trill, dies, and her symbiont Dax is transferred to a new host, Ezri. It is taboo in Trill society for a joined Trill to form relationships with partners or spouses of former hosts of their symbiont, or, put differently, from their past lives. Therefore, Ezri Dax is forbidden from becoming romantically involved with Worf, Jadzia's widower. Ezri does it anyway, starting a relationship with Worf, in defiance of Trill norms.

As it turns out, Ezri and Worf find their relationship to be transient. Both of them, it appears, have moved beyond the relationship after Dax was joined with Ezri. Neither Dax nor Worf is the same as before.

A protégé who has had several mentors in some ways is like a joined Trill. Like a joined Trill, a protégé carries all the experience and memories of the previous mentor–protégé experience, but the protégé is an evolved person with a personality combining past and present, old and new. Going back to a former mentor has the appeal of offering the certainty that was once felt with the former mentor.

However, once a mentor relationship has ended or evolved into another kind of relationship, it is no longer the same. The protégé is no longer the same either. Revisiting the relationship with an old mentor may be unsatisfying. The mentor may no longer be the same source of guidance as he was in a previous time. The protégé and mentor may remain colleagues, like Ezri and Worf, but the previous relationship has passed.

6.7 The three degrees of mentors

Good mentors are habit forming. You might want to have more than one.

How many mentors is too many? That is like asking how many handbags are too many. Some people, like my mother, have a small number of great bags which are perfect for all occasions. Other people, like the Kardashians, have entire closets built for their bags, of which they may use several in the course of a day. A protégé's needs (either for a bag or a mentor!) can vary widely.

Different stages of a career call for different mentors, and there are at least three stages of anyone's career. In the art world, these stages are "emerging," "mid-career," and "established." These labels are equally applicable to careers outside the art world as well.

My friends, artist Miriam Cabessa and sculptor Fred Eversley, are each considered established artists. Their works are recognized and sold internationally, including at Christie's and Sotheby's. However, at an earlier stage, they were in mid-career — they each had a body of independent work and had been presented at exhibitions, but had not yet gotten attention from major art critics or publications. Even earlier, when they were much younger and not well known, they were regarded as emerging.

Implicit in the label "emerging" is the expectation that the artist will, in fact, emerge. The label is an inherent affirmation. It is also euphemistic: "emerging" is much more appealing than "unknown." It would be hard to attract the public to an exhibition of an artist touted as "inexperienced and unknown." In every emerging artist, there is an established artist dying to get out.

Other professionals — doctors, lawyers, accountants, teachers, journalists, architects, engineers, and others — have the same three stages of their careers. As with artists, the dividing lines can be grey.

How important are financial criteria in determining whether a person is "established"? Can you be considered "established" even if you are unsuccessful financially, have no clients or patrons, or are unemployed? Is a person "established" only if others see him that way?

How does this relate to mentors? In identifying the right mentor, it's useful to know whether you are emerging, mid-career, or established.

People at all three levels benefit from a mentor, but the types of mentor for each level is different. An emerging professional might benefit most from a mentor who can open doors to jobs or show them the ropes when in a job. A mentor for a mid-career professional may open doors to clients or niche areas of their industry. A mentor for an established professional may provide highly sophisticated guidance in pursuing C-suite positions or political appointments.

One caution: labels can be limiting — even self-labelling. For that reason, labels should generally be avoided. While self-labelling can be helpful for the limited purpose of identifying what kind of mentor can help you get ahead, it's important never to be owned by your label.

PART 7

Overheard Conversations

PART 7:

Overheard Conversations

7.1 A trailblazing architect

Taylor is the protégé of Ivana, an architect who is widely regarded as a visionary in Manhattan real estate. I interviewed Taylor about what it is like being Ivana's protégé.

Your mentor Ivana is noted for her commitment to the environment. What were the factors that drew you to your mentor? What matters most to you?

Ivana is the real deal. She doesn't put up a façade of what some people expect an architect to be like. She never pretends to be something she is not. She is more of an artist, or at least more in touch with the artistic side of architecture. By being true to herself, she influences me to be true to myself as well.

Can you give me an example of how her authenticity is manifested in her work?

She doesn't design new buildings; she restores old ones. Since she was a child, Ivana had a love for old buildings. She would collect photographs of buildings in Manhattan that she thought were particularly beautiful or interesting. You can't fake that — as an architect and designer, this has to be in your core. She makes me get in touch with the things that drew me to architecture to start with. In my case, my childhood obsession with Lego sets. She put me in touch with my architectural child. Now I think about Legos when I'm working on a design.

As an emerging architect, does your mentor's relationship to the designs of the past ever impair your ability to envision something totally new?

She reconciles the two and has shown me how to do so as well. Old architecture is beautiful but not always practical in the present time. That's where a new vision comes in. Ivana is innovative, and she brings my innovation to the front. She gives my creativity a lot of oxygen. If I have a jumble of ideas, she sees which ones are fresh and non-derivative, and focuses me on these. She doesn't come right out and say, "Taylor, that idea is mundane" — she just picks up on the good ideas and lets the others float away.

Your mentor's leadership on environmental issues is notable in the community. She has been described as "green to the extreme." How has that affected you as her protégé?

Her unrelenting commitment to sustainability is one of the principal things that drew me to her. Because if we don't all commit to a sustainable environment, we won't have an environment. Ivana led me to see that, by prioritizing sustainability, you can influence the very way that people want to live.

This is an important issue to your generation, as it should be to all generations. Are there any specific examples of things you have learned from her along the way that have impacted you?

Ivana used reclaimed wood and recycled nails in a high-end urban condo. She is attempting to build a net-zero impact project in Manhattan. That means a building which does not consume more energy than it produces, so that its net carbon footprint is zero. Do you have any idea of how hard that is — how much resistance there is to this? Sometimes when faced with something that she feels is necessary, but that seems daunting, infeasible, or downright impossible — she says, "I'm just going to do it anyway."

Ivana has restored some historically significant buildings. This has been the focus of her work much more than new developments. How has this affected your development as an emerging architect?

The characteristic that she has honed in me is the ability to weave old elements and historical references into my work. Selectively. Not indiscriminate nostalgia, but a curated approach to the past.

Your mentor clearly loves the architecture of the Nineteenth Century but you seem more drawn to the Twentieth.

I am, but her relationship with the 1800s has helped me with the 1900s as well. She helps me see "mid-century" in a different way. It's not all fabulous. Some of it was bad at the time; now it is old and bad. The thing about having a great mentor is that her vision starts rubbing off on you. You start to be able to see things in a clearer, better way.

7.2 A young entrepreneur

I interviewed Kasie, a new entrant in the fashion industry, who launched a women's apparel line four years ago. We talked about her mentor, Ciara.

Who did you turn to for advice when you were getting started?

It was very hard to get good advice, and to separate good advice from bad. There was no built-in method for finding a mentor in this field. I was jealous of my friends in law firms or large companies that had senior people they could approach. Fortunately, I did find someone I could talk to early on. Ironically, she was a competitor, Ciara.

Your mentor, Ciara, had launched a similar business only three years before you launched yours. Having recently been in your very situation, what kind of advice did she give you?

Ciara was remarkably on point with her advice. She told me two things that virtually saved me from going out of business in the first two years. Her best advice was, "Do not get overwhelmed. Keep your focus on what you set out to do. Break it down day by day. Do what you can get done each day. Don't try to move everything forward at once." She also said, "Whenever you feel like you are going to fail, remember what brought you here to start with and hold that thought. Be flexible, but don't let anyone get you off your path or your plan."

Was there a time that those words made the difference in what you did or didn't do, and can you describe what it was?

As you know, my vision was simple: contemporary classic capsule suiting pieces in basic colors for young professional women.

Everything washable and packable at a good price point. My first collection was an epic struggle in itself to produce. There were only two stores that were willing to order from me. One store sent half of the order back and didn't order for the next season — she told me her customers saw the pieces as "too dowdy." The other store never paid for the clothes, and I didn't have the money to sue them! It was awful, but I learned a lot.

How did you keep from giving up?

I remember calling Ciara at a point when I was so discouraged, I was wondering if I should give up the entire venture. She talked me off the ledge! She told me that the first store would eventually want me back and that the second store would go out of business in a year. She was right. She hadn't dealt with either store because the first store was a bit out of her geography and thus she hadn't approached them. As to the second store, she didn't like the owner and didn't want to deal with her. I felt that I had been too trusting and should have walked away like Ciara did. She said, "This wasn't your mistake, it was theirs. Never punish yourself. Never look back. Don't let them throw you off your path."

Easier said than done. How did you stay on the path at the beginning, when you were losing money and no one was paying you?

Ciara told me a story that helped me get through the day when I was feeling that things were hopeless. Her second year in business, she managed to get a deal with a department store, one of the largest and most prestigious stores in the country. This could be a breakthrough for her and set her up for years to come. However, a few months in, she found the store extraordinarily difficult to deal with. The store's demands would fundamentally change her line in a way that didn't represent her vision. Finally, she decided she had had it and fired them as a client. A few minutes later, she was having a panic attack over what she'd done. She told me her hands were shaking, but she kept her resolve. Eventually, it ended up being the best thing she ever did. She told me, "Don't give anyone too much power in your head. The most important person to you is you."

That is amazing advice. Some said you were entering an already saturated niche market of selling basic dresses for career women. It's a highly competitive industry. Did you ask Ciara if she thought there was room in the market for one more, that is, you?

I did, and her answer startled me. She said, "No one else believes this, but there is safety in numbers. We each do better if the other one succeeds, because we will both expand the market for the other."

What was it about Ciara that made her a mentor, rather than simply a friend or a sounding board?

She was able to see something in me that others did not. I had an economics and finance background, but what she saw in me instead was an echo of my ancestry. My great-grandparents had worked in the garment industry in Italy. In fact, my father was the first person in his family to work outside of the clothing industry in 500 years. Ciara picked up on a deeply imbedded characteristic of mine — a certain affinity for fabric and style — that no one else recognized. You could say that she put me in touch with my own DNA.

I appreciate that she doesn't just see me as another one of her. She understands what I am good at and what I am not. Her background, unlike mine, is in design. She knows that sometimes the design side of this is challenging for me and that I'm not always able to gauge trends. She is able to point me in the right direction so that I can learn what I need to learn.

Ciara has gotten an enormous amount of publicity over the past two years. People seem obsessed with her. What accounts for this?

She's a visionary in many ways. Her perspective is remarkable. Of course, I see and experience this on a direct, personal level. She gives me insight that I don't get from anyone else.

In retrospect, do you feel that you were limited in any way by having a young mentor? Stating this differently, how might you have benefited from the advice of someone more experienced?

Ciara was a perfect mentor. A more seasoned veteran of the fashion industry would have been too negative or would have based advice on prevailing assumptions at the time, which we now know are not true. Before I launched the business, I heard that what I wanted to do couldn't be done: that the women's apparel market is too competitive, that there is no way to make quality at this price point, and that the marketing alone will be too expensive. I'm glad I didn't listen to someone older or more experienced!

This is a great story. Do you think you and Ciara will ever go into business together?

Interesting that you should ask. For a while, we've been discussing a collaboration. As you know, her line is more upscale and fashion-forward than mine, which is affordable, tailored capsule pieces. We are working on a limited edition of affordable fashion-forward pieces with designs by each of us. We're calling it "Ciara x Kasie."

7.3 An emerging artist

Freja is the protégé of Erika, an established artist. We talked about Erika in Freja's studio.

You have one of the most unusual mentors of your generation of artists. How did that relationship come about?

It was somewhat accidental. There are programs to connect young artists with mentors who were established artists, but I wasn't interested in applying. I wanted to learn from someone, but I didn't want the relationship to be imposed on me in that way.

Your mentor is quite a bit older than you. I am not sure but I think she is in her mid-70s and you are under 30?

I haven't asked her how old she is but I believe she is older than my parents. My parents, by the way, were instrumental in my meeting Erika. I went with them to a wine-and-cheese event at the home of one of our neighbors in Soho, a sculptor and his architect wife. Several other Soho artists were there, including Erika. I talked to her for a long time. It was a really interesting conversation, and she invited me to her studio.

Artists don't extend studio invitations to everyone.

She may have invited me initially because my parents were friends and neighbors. There are very few parents in the neighborhood, so they all try to help each other's kids. While that may have accounted for the first invitation, I asked her why she let me continue to work with her in her studio. She said that she picked up in our first conversation that I had a certain technique to my work which was unique, and she sensed I had potential.

You get down on your hands and knees on the floor, kneeling in the middle of the canvas. You use a variety of unusual media — things that other people might view as trash.

Yes, that is what I do. It's different from how Erika works — she works in a more traditional fashion using acrylic on an upright canvas — and she was intrigued by what I was doing. I am not sure that I realized it at the time, but as I spent more time with her, I started to see how my technique is a unique driver of my art.

Your work is very different from what you did in the early part of your career. How did Erika influence that?

As an artist, your work is supposed to be provocative as well as evocative. That is fine in the abstract, but it's in the execution that things can get very confused. She showed me how to provoke and evoke.

Erika's work might not exactly be called provocative, but it is certainly impactful. How did she teach you to be provocative?

I would say that she didn't tell me; she showed me. She had me bring over projects and we would talk and work on them together. At first, I had no idea what I was doing. I would start a piece with a shocking image or concept — like a lithograph of a politician, over which I would splatter red paint, to suggest blood on his hands — and then I wouldn't know where to go with it. She would suggest watering it down little by little, so that the provocation was subtle. Maybe the entire picture became tinged with red. To paraphrase your words, she worked on it until it was impactful, not shocking. I watched her work in a similar fashion with her own canvases for many hours.

A famous artist mentor has said that a protégé is influenced by how the mentor operates. How does Erika operate?

Sometimes in ways that were new and unexpected. Sometimes in ways that were old and unexpected. She would start with the concept of a paradigm shift — an image that was masculine would become feminine, for example. But then she would take the work in a direction I wouldn't have expected. I saw this again and again. She had an expression for this: "Knock over the board."

As in, the third option in a chess game?

Yes, exactly. She showed me how to find the third option — the equivalent of turning the board upside down. This has become the driving principle of my work.

7.4 A charismatic celebrity

Ryan is the protégé of Jonathan, one of the most famous lawyers in America. We talked about his experience with a celebrity mentor.

What was it like to have a rock star as a mentor?

It took me a long time not to be a bit starstruck by him. I was a bit intimidated by him at first. I quickly got over that. Now I sometimes forget who he is.

You would not be the only one to be impressed with him. One commentator called him "the most profound legal talent of our time." How did you come to be his protégé? Did you seek him out — the most profound legal talent of our time?

I was told that it was important for me that he know who I was. I introduced myself to him at a conference. Years later, I called him and asked him to lunch. It was a lunch that changed my life.

I recall that you were making your mark at the time and had been tapped to chair a significant justice reform project for the bar association.

In fact, the lunch and the bar project were related. The project was a nationwide-wide study on individuals' experience with the legal system, which I was asked to spearhead. It was getting a lot of media attention. I needed advice and direction.

I would think that he had some controversial opinions about the subject. He's known as a cheerleader for the legal system. One commentator has referred to him as "the American justice system's number one apologist."

Yes, I'm getting to that. I remember everything about that lunch. Jonathan ordered the mushroom risotto. I did the same, because he had ordered it. I think I was just too fascinated by him to focus on the menu.

Okay, so food selection was the first advice you got from him. What did he say about your bar association project?

One of my premises was that the public had largely lost confidence in the justice system. He told me that I was flat out wrong and that both the legal system and public confidence in it were strong. I said that our surveys indicated just the opposite. He said, "Your surveys are wrong. You need to change the premise of your report."

Given your mandate to report findings, how did you react to his telling you that your conclusions — based on your survey data — were wrong?

I was rattled by it. He said to me, "You have an opportunity to influence the direction of the legal system and public opinion on this issue. The impact of the report for generations to come should be your overarching concern." He did not see ignoring the survey data as dishonest; he believed the survey data was wrong. On the other hand, I saw the data as the data. I could choose to contextualize it or criticize it, but I couldn't change it or deny it.

Did you follow his advice?

You will have to read my report to find out. The lunch was a turning point for me. It set the stage for our entire relationship, and defined my view of him and what it meant to have him as a mentor. In the course of one lunch, I went from being in awe of him and ready to follow his every word, to questioning something he was quite emphatic about.

How could you see him as a mentor, given that the first thing he told you to do was something you disagreed with? I guess it was actually the second thing he told you — the first one was to try the risotto.

Yes, and he was right about the risotto. As to the second thing, the exchange we had at that lunch made me understand his world view. It enabled me to view his advice in the context of that world view. He has an unshakable belief in the justice system, the way he has an unshakable certainly about everything. I realized that confidence in institutions is not my world view. In my mind, all major institutions have been tarnished: governments, political leaders, universities, corporations, and religious institutions. Jonathan feels the issues that I see are merely temporary blips and that all of these institutions remain strong. In spite of fundamental differences in our perspectives, I value his views. He was making a point about the survey — publication would have consequences, which in his view outweighed the value of the disclosure. It just wasn't a point that I happened to agree with. Hearing his view, however, caused me to see my role in an entirely new way — the role of an influencer. He made me see that it was my responsibility to balance the harm I might be creating — by publishing a survey suggesting lack of public confidence in the justice system — with the benefit of such a disclosure. He caused me to ask questions that I didn't ask before.

That is truly remarkable. Do you feel you were cheated out of the full "celebrity mentor" experience because it started on a note of dissonance?

Not at all. There is a point in every protégé's relationship with a mentor where the protégé has to grow up and not act like a kid trying to please a parent. I consider myself lucky that I got to that point so quickly.

Can you describe how your relationship with Jonathan progressed after this?

I would contact him from time to time to run something by him. A few years ago, I questioned whether I was at the right firm. I was considering a move to a different firm. Jonathan talked me into staying where I was. In his words, "Your career is what you make it. Your legal life is independent of any one firm." He made me see that it's easier to tap resources in a familiar setting with established relationships, than it is to start from scratch at a new firm. He was very direct with me — something no one else was.

Did you ever collaborate with him on a case?

Unfortunately, I never had the opportunity. I did watch him argue cases from time to time and was highly influenced by that.

Jonathan's courtroom advocacy is singular. One legal writer called him a "force of nature." What did you learn from watching him in court?

In one of his recent cases, he boldly, unabashedly, argued for a radical departure from existing law and procedure, based on the exigencies of the particular case. He told the court that international financial systems would be permanently damaged if the court weren't flexible and didn't depart from existing precedent.

He may have been the only person who could have told a court to do something so bold. He had the stature, the standing, the credibility.

He was, and he persuaded the court. This is why I have listened to him time and time again when he told me what to do. I generally don't listen to anybody, but I listen to him. It's very ill-advised not to listen to him because he is always right.

No one is always right. Did you ever experience another instance when he was wrong, other than the very initial advice he gave you, when he told you to ignore your survey results?

Not really. The reason his advice is always so good is the same reason the first advice was so bad: his optimism. He fueled my optimism, and in doing that, he led me to engineer my own success. He didn't allow me to indulge the idea of failure. He always thought he would succeed. He didn't consider the possibility that I would fail either. He had a moral certainty about it, which emboldened me. I had faith in him and he was certain I would succeed. That's the vision and certainty of a true mentor.

7.5 Protégé roundtable: a critique of the mentors

Stephanie: Freja, Kasie, Ryan and Taylor, I'm going to put all of you on the spot and ask you to critique your mentors. They are never going to read this interview so I ask that you be as candid as possible. Kasie, first of all, let me ask you: were there any times that you were frustrated with Ciara as a mentor?

Kasie: I wished she could have given me more practical, direct help. She was a great cheerleader, and she often gave me inspiring soundbites, but she could not relate completely to my struggles. She had more funding starting out than I did, because she had independent sources of income. I did not have her safety net. Even though she knew that, it was hard for her to understand the limitations I was facing. She was not in a position to give any guidance as to how to grow a business without a safety net, because she had always had one.

Stephanie: Do you wish you had had a mentor who, perhaps, had started out with less start-up capital, and perhaps may have better understood what it was like?

Kasie: That's a hard question. Our conversation didn't get bogged down in a discussion of the financial risk of failure. Perhaps another mentor might have made me focus more on avoiding risk, a focus that did not need to be magnified for me. Ciara was able to see only the upside, which is a side I had trouble focusing on. She was able to steer me toward the best long-term decisions instead of the most risk-averse ones.

Stephanie: Taylor, was there anything you wished Ivana would have done differently as a mentor?

Taylor: Sometimes she was too busy to talk or meet when I needed guidance or advice. I can't really complain about this, as she had her own business she was running, which had priority. On balance, however, the time spent with her was always worth waiting for. When I had her attention, she was there 100%.

Ryan: I was so star struck by Jonathan, and so grateful for the time he did give me, that it never occurred to me to critique him as a mentor. I was always stunned by his willingness to talk to me, have lunch with me, or read my draft articles. Was there anything about him that I found frustrating? His propensity to see things in black and white. There was no ambiguity with him. He was extraordinarily definite, something that to this day I cannot completely understand.

Stephanie: Freja, what do you wish had been different with Erika?

Freja: I wish she were younger. I felt that the age gap was so great, she was like someone from another world. On the other hand, her insight and innovativeness were like no one I had ever met. It was more that I felt the information gap between us was so great.

Stephanie: Do any of you wish you had done anything differently as a protégé?

Taylor: I wish I had used the time I had with Ivana to observe more and tap into her brain more. I feel that I could have absorbed more if I had just been more prepared and had asked more questions.

Ryan: I should have asked more questions, probed more. I could have asked Jonathan "why" a bit more.

Kasie: I wish I had spent more time with Ciara. We had long text conversations, but looking back, I could have gone over to her workshop more. I may have picked up more by being there with her as she was working — seeing her in her natural habitat, so to speak.

Ryan: I agree. I never was in Jonathan's office.

Freja: I feel the same way as Taylor — I wish I had been more observant and tried to absorb more of Erika's process and format.

Stephanie: What advice would you give a protégé about how to get the most from a mentor?

Ryan: Ask questions. Don't be reticent. Don't idolize them. Don't follow them blindly. Sometimes they can be wrong.

Taylor: Observe everything. Try to absorb as much as you can.

Kasie: Make the effort to have in-person meetings, at least once in a while.

Freja: Don't be afraid that you are imposing on them or their time.

7.6 Impossible conversation with a dead mentor

Stephanie: Thank you for speaking with me today. Can I ask you, why have you agreed to come back from the dead and do this interview?

Robert: I didn't realize it when I was alive, but I miss the experience of being a mentor. Call it nostalgia.

Stephanie: I miss it too, although I have had other mentors since you passed away. Each one is different and has his own place. Which brings me to my first question: what was it like for you having a female protégé for the first time?

Robert: It was different from what I expected. I had had other women students who had promise, but never one who was as determined and intent on success. You took my advice seriously, I was not expecting that, or, frankly, used to it.

Stephanie: I was very eager to please you. I was a little scared of you.

Robert: I didn't know you were scared of me — you didn't seem scared of anything or anyone.

Stephanie: I'm glad I put up a good front.

Robert: Indeed.

Stephanie: You gave me excellent guidance, even when I didn't follow it. Although I think I almost always did. How did you know when to give me advice, what advice to give, and how to give it?

Robert: That's a lot of questions. What advice to give? That's an easy one. I saw your capabilities and disposition, and it seemed obvious to me what you should do. When did I offer advice? When you asked me for it (laughter).

Stephanie: I remember once you offered advice when I did not ask for it: you told me I should break up with Joe.

Robert: I didn't tell you to break up with him — I just told you I didn't see what you were doing with him. And I saw my other teaching assistant, Peter, being a better match for you.

Stephanie: One of my best friends liked Peter. I was not about to cross swords.

Robert: Well, that is a quality that has suited you well in your legal career — loyalty.

Stephanie: I was struggling with how to find a job after law school, and you urged me to pursue judicial clerkships. That had not occurred to me and did not seem in the realm of the possible. How did you know to guide me there?

Robert: A federal clerkship suited your personality and served your ultimate career path. It was the logical route to pursue. And I was able to help, since I knew many of the judges personally and could offer a recommendation.

Stephanie: Would you have done this for any student who asked?

Robert: Absolutely not. I was certain you would succeed. You were determined. Again and again, I watched you succeed at whatever you had determined to do. I had a vested interest in your legal career.

Stephanie: You continued to help me after I graduated. You asked me to go to events with you where there were important networking opportunities for me.

Robert: It was actually my wife's idea. She is a lawyer but she hates these types of events. She said, why don't you take that former student of yours who is a bankruptcy lawyer?

Stephanie: It was nice of her. I guess that mentoring is sometimes a family affair.

Robert: As a woman lawyer in an era where there were very few, she was most supportive of women law students.

Stephanie: Was mentoring a woman different for you than mentoring a man?

Robert: It was. You were more open to receiving advice than the men I have mentored. But I treaded more carefully, too. I was not sure what your personal goals were and how that would affect your career. For instance, I didn't know if you wanted a husband or a family. And I certainly was not about to ask. I chose to simply give the advice I would give regardless of these considerations. If it didn't suit you, I guess you would tell me or disregard my advice.

Stephanie: Was there any advice you would have given to me if you felt that marriage or family were a priority?

Robert: Maybe, if I thought you were moving to Newark, New Jersey to marry — what's his name — I wouldn't have seen you as able to relocate. I might not have urged you to apply for clerkships outside of the Newark area. If you had settled down and had children at that point, I might not have urged you to pursue the Justice Department position after your clerkship, since it would be in Washington, D.C. and much travel is involved. I might have presumed that you would be unable to move or that the travel would conflict with your family life. On reflection, I'm not sure what I would have told you, I would have loathed watering down my advice or suggesting that you not pursue the best career opportunities, wherever located.

Stephanie: I feel you always gave me good advice, even on the one occasion I didn't follow it. Is there any advice that you wish you had given me that you hadn't?

Robert: I might have told you to undertake more writing projects earlier or to get involved with more professional groups at an earlier juncture.

Stephanie: I think you probably did tell me those things. I would have done well to do them. I guess on balance though, I did listen to you on the big things.

Robert: You did.

Stephanie: Thank you for taking the time to do this interview with me. It's been a rare pleasure. I hope you have a nice eternity.

Robert: Thank you. The same to you.

PART 8
Nuts and bolts

PART 8:

Nuts and bolts

8.1 Mentor etiquette

The mentor–protégé relationship is unique and, as such, has its own rules of etiquette. Obviously, each situation is different. The answers to questions below are only intended as general guidelines.

Is it appropriate or expected that I give my mentor gifts?

This depends on your relationship with your mentor. Generally, you should give your mentor a gift only if the context requires. For example, if the mentor invites you to his wedding, a gift is appropriate. Sometimes spontaneous gifts such as books are also appropriate. However, it is not necessary or appropriate to give gifts for holidays or birthdays.

Who pays for lunch?

You should offer to pick up the check the first time. However, if your mentor insists on picking it up, you should graciously thank him and insist that he allow you to pick it up or split it next time.

What do I do if my mentor asks me to help with a project or attend an event, and I don't want to accept? How do I decline an invitation or request from my mentor?

You are his protégé, not his employee or his child. You can simply decline politely as you would with a friend or colleague.

How do I tell my mentor I want something from him, such as a letter of recommendation or help with a project?

Tell him you have a favor to ask. Most likely, he will be happy to oblige.

Should I ask my mentor for a large favor that might be an imposition on him?

As a general rule, it's appropriate to ask for a favor, but it is not appropriate to impose. The difference between the two is an objective test: would most people consider the request a favor or an imposition? For example, you should never ask your mentor to loan you money. Most people would regard lending money as an imposition. On the other hand, if your apartment is being renovated and your mentor has a guest house, asking to stay in the guest house for a few days is a favor (provided, of course, that you leave the place spotless). Asking for a job recommendation is not an imposition and is never an inappropriate request of a mentor.

Should I invite my mentor to my wedding?

It depends on your relationship with your mentor, but generally you should, particularly if it is a large wedding and you are inviting other professional colleagues.

Should I tell my mentor that I disagree with advice he has given me?

No. His advice is a gift, and it is ungracious to tell someone that you don't like his gift. You certainly should not, however, follow advice you deem to be poor. Moreover, receiving bad advice from him may be a sign that your relationship with him as a mentor has run its course.

How do I tell my mentor that he is engaging in self-destructive behavior?

It not your responsibility to intervene. You are his protégé, not his parent or therapist. If his behavior is so risky, however, that it threatens his life or someone else's, you may be obliged to intervene, but once you do so, you can no longer be his protégé. The situation will effectively end your relationship as mentor-protégé, as your intervention will fundamentally alter your relationship.

What should I do if my mentor is exploiting me?

This depends on the degree and frequency of the exploitation. Is your mentor asking you to babysit for his children, or is he expecting you to ghostwrite articles for him? Is it occasional or chronic?

Asking a protégé for help or favors once in a while is not exploitation. The mentor–protégé relationship is not a one-way street, and some reciprocity in the relationship is appropriate. However, if the request is intrusive or makes you uncomfortable, you should decline. If he persists, this may be a sign that the mentor–protégé relationship needs to end.

My mentor asked me to dinner. I am unsure if this is a date. What should I do?

If you would like to have dinner with him, you should. You should assume it is not a date unless he gives you a reason to think otherwise.

My mentor made a sexual advance. What should I do?

A boundary has been crossed. Regardless of what happens next, the mentor–protégé relationship has now been altered and may even be over. As to what you should do in response, this is a complex question, for which the following decision tree may be helpful.

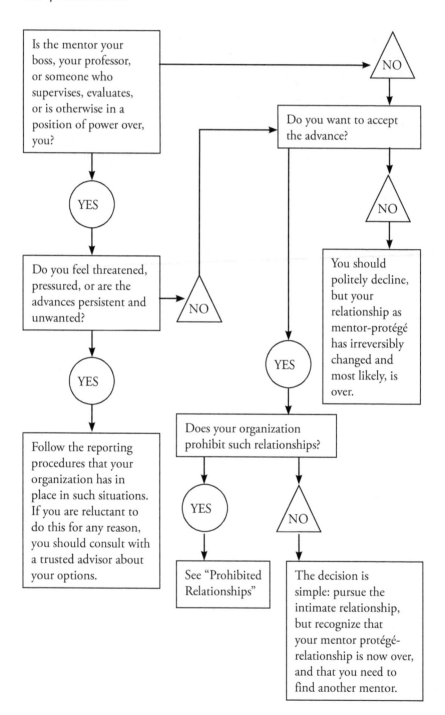

Is the mentor your boss, your professor, or someone who supervises, evaluates, or is otherwise in a position of power over, you?

NO

Do you want to accept the advance?

NO

YES

Do you feel threatened, pressured, or are the advances persistent and unwanted?

NO

You should politely decline, but your relationship as mentor-protégé has irreversibly changed and most likely, is over.

YES

YES

Follow the reporting procedures that your organization has in place in such situations. If you are reluctant to do this for any reason, you should consult with a trusted advisor about your options.

Does your organization prohibit such relationships?

YES

NO

See "Prohibited Relationships"

The decision is simple: pursue the intimate relationship, but recognize that your mentor protégé-relationship is now over, and that you need to find another mentor.

Prohibited relationships

For some, the fact that a relationship is prohibited will make the decision not to pursue the relationship clear. For others, the decision may be less clear. Some may regard the rules prohibiting the relationship as intrusive or feel that the rules may be broken if the circumstances warrant. Others may feel that such a relationship takes priority over all other considerations.

An organization's rules regarding workplace relationships are created in the interest of the organization as a whole. Relationships between employees and supervisors, or students and professors, impact not just those in the relationship, but others in their organization as well. For example, such relationships inevitably create conflicts of interest or the perception of unfairness in the evaluation process. These effects can damage the organization.

Violating the rules may have severe consequences to the individuals involved, including discharge or termination. If you chose to break a rule, you need to be aware of the potential consequences and decide if the intimate relationship is important enough to you to warrant the risk.

What is the best way to thank a mentor who has helped you immeasurably?

There is no one way to thank a mentor. You can take him to lunch and tell him, "Thank you." You can send him a plant with a card. You can write a book and dedicate it to him. You can do just about anything, in fact, to thank someone who was a great mentor to you.

There is no wrong way to thank your Mentor X.

CPSIA information can be obtained
at www.ICGtesting.com
Printed in the USA
LVHW081242150819
627730LV00006BA/52/P